THE HUMAN BRAIN IN 30 SECONDS

First published in the UK in 2016 by Ivy Kids.
This edition published in the US in 2018 by

Ivy Kids

An imprint of The Quarto Group
The Old Brewery
6 Blundell Street
London N7 9BH
United Kingdom
www.QuartoKnows.com

Copyright © 2017 Quarto Publishing plc

All rights reserved. No part of this book may be reproduced or transmitted in any form or by any means, electronic or mechanical, including photocopying, recording, or by any information storage-and-retrieval system, without written permission from the copyright holder.

ISBN: 978-1-78240-612-9

This book was conceived, designed & produced by

Ivy Kids

58 West Street, Brighton BN1 2RA, United Kingdom

PUBLISHER	Susan Kelly
CREATIVE DIRECTOR	Michael Whitehead
COMMISSIONING EDITOR	Hazel Songhurst
MANAGING EDITOR	Susie Behar
PROJECT EDITOR	Cath Senker
ART DIRECTOR	Hanri van Wyk
DESIGNER	Claire Munday
DESIGN ASSISTANT	Emily Hurlock
EDITORIAL ASSISTANT	Lucy Menzies

Printed in China

1 3 5 7 9 10 8 6 4 2

THE HUMAN BRAIN
IN 30 SECONDS

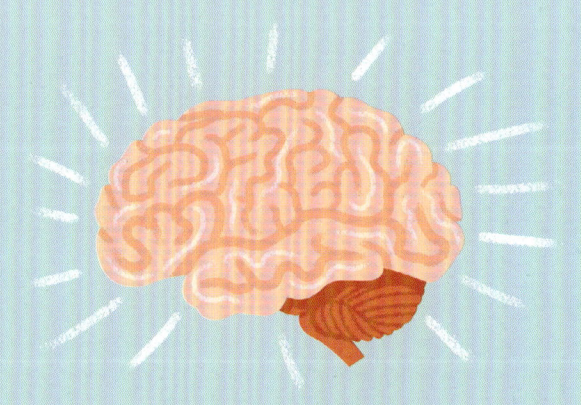

CLIVE GIFFORD

ILLUSTRATED BY WESLEY ROBINS
CONSULTANT: PROFESSOR ANIL SETH

IVY KIDS

Contents

About this book 6

MEET YOUR BRAIN 8
Glossary 10
Brain box 12
Parts of the brain 14
Lots of lobes 16
Brain hemispheres 18
Imaging the brain 20
The hungry brain 22

GETTING CONNECTED 24
Glossary 26
Sending signals 28
Making connections 30
Bundle of nerves 32
Reflexes 34
The endocrine system 36

MAKING SENSE 38
Glossary 40
Taste and smell 42
Hearing 44
Sight 46
Touch and other senses 48
Perception 50
Taking shortcuts 52

MEMORY 54
Glossary 56
Making memories 58
Long-term memory 60
Forgetting 62
Memory aids 64

EMOTIONS 66
Glossary 68
What are emotions? 70
Fight or flight 72
Sleep and dreams 74

BRAIN SKILLS 76
Glossary 78
Types of intelligence 80
Language intelligence 82
Visual-spatial intelligence 84
Logic and problem-solving 86
Creativity and invention 88
Artificial intelligence 90
Discover more 92

Index 94
Answers 96

About this book
... in 60 seconds

Most parts of your body are designed to perform just one task. For example, your heart is a powerful pump, driving blood around your body. Your brain, in contrast, is a marvelous, multitasking miracle!

For starters, it controls almost all of the many parts of your body, sending out instructions to muscles and joints every time you move. It monitors and controls how your body's systems are working, such as the speed of your breathing and your heart rate.

Your brain also deals with the constant flood of information sent to it by your senses. It filters, organizes, and acts on the signals it receives. Your clever brain allows you to remember situations, facts, and skills stored in your memory—months or years later. It also enables you to react quickly to events, to think and make decisions, to plan ahead, solve problems, and gather knowledge in many different ways.

And it does all of these things almost all of the time. Your busy, busy brain barely slows down, even when you're asleep. Whew!

This book whisks you and your brain through a range of mind-blowing topics. It looks at what actually happens inside your head, how the brain works, how it deals with and stores information, and how it helps make you who you are.

Each topic has a page to read as fast or slow as you like, and a speedy summary to give you the vital facts in seconds. The illustrations give you the information in an easy-to-grasp, visual way.

Activities and experiments throughout the book encourage you to play brain detective, and investigate the object that Nobel Prize-winning scientist David H. Hubel described as "like nothing else we know of in the universe."

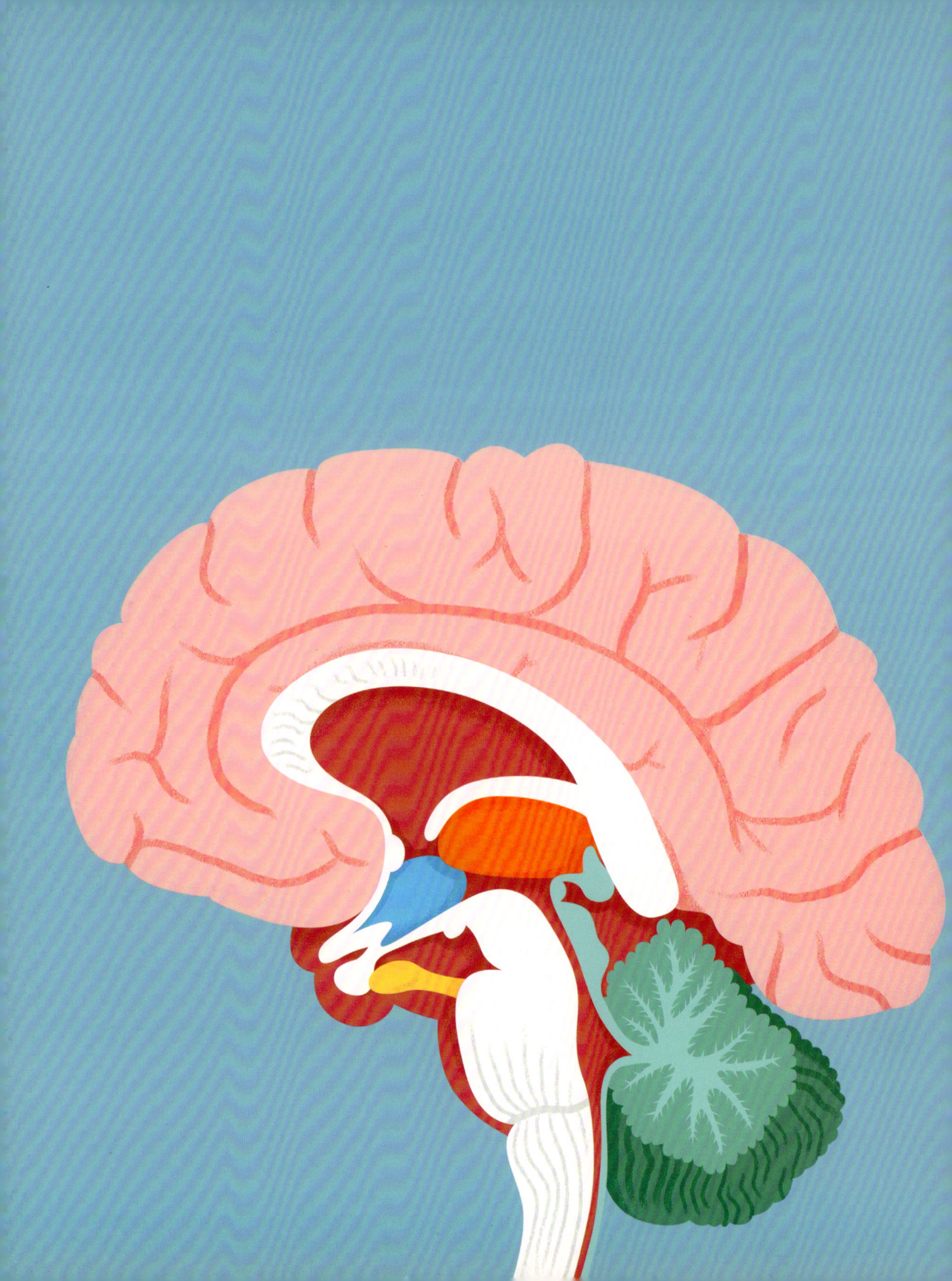

Meet your brain

Everything you do, think, and feel, and all your body parts that keep you alive are controlled by something that looks a little like a whitish-gray cauliflower. Your brain weighs approximately 3 lb (1.4 kg), about three times the weight of a chimpanzee's brain and over five times the weight of a lion's. It may not look impressive from the outside, but your brain is an extraordinary powerhouse of activity that needs looking after!

Meet your brain
Glossary

amygdala A small, almond-shaped part, deep in the brain, that is involved with emotions and memory.

brain stem The lower part of the brain that connects to the spinal cord.

cell One of the tiny units that make up living things. The human body consists of millions and millions of cells of different types.

cerebellum The part of the brain that coordinates your body's movements and keeps you balanced.

cerebrospinal fluid A clear liquid that surrounds the brain inside the skull and protects and nourishes it.

cerebrum The largest part of the brain, responsible for handling memories, thoughts, and feelings, and senses such as touch.

coordinate To make the different parts of your body work well together.

corpus callosum A large bundle of nerves that connect the right and left halves of the brain.

cortex Also known as the cerebral cortex, this is the surface layer of the cerebrum.

EEG Short for electro-encephalogram, this is a medical test used to record electrical activity in the brain.

glucose The main type of sugar made by the body from food. It is carried through the bloodstream to provide energy to the cells of the body.

hypothalamus A small but vital part of the brain that performs a range of jobs, including helping to control sleep, thirst, and body temperature.

meninges Sheets of tissue that cover the brain and help protect it.

MRI Short for Magnetic Resonance Imaging, this is a way of examining brain activity by observing changes in the amount of blood flow and oxygen carried around the brain.

nerves A bundle of long fibers made up of nerve cells. Most nerves carry signals to and from the brain.

oxygen A gas that is taken in from air during breathing and carried around the body in the bloodstream. Oxygen is essential for the body to release energy from food.

spinal cord A thick bundle of nerve fibers that runs from the base of the brain through the spine and that allows the brain to control the body.

thalamus Part of the brain that relays signals from the senses to other parts of the brain and connects different parts of the cortex together.

three dimensions (3D) If you can see things in 3D, you can see they have not only height and width, but also depth.

tissue A collection of cells that form the different parts of humans, animals, and plants.

voluntary To do something that you want to do, and are aware of wanting to do, such as moving your hand to pick something up.

Brain box
... in 30 seconds

Thinking may sometimes be hard, but your brain is soft and squishy. It feels a little like tofu or jelly. Something that soft could easily get damaged out in the open, so fortunately your brain has several layers of protection.

Your brain sits inside a large bony skull. This is made up of eight different plates of bone, together called the cranium, as well as the bones that form your face. Wrapped around the brain are three sheets of tissue called meninges. The outer one, the dura mater, is especially tough. Together, these tissues help protect the brain.

Your brain is always swimming. It floats in around 4½–5½ oz (130–160 ml) of liquid called cerebrospinal fluid. This cushions it like a shock absorber and makes the brain lighter, so you don't have all 3 lb (1.4 kg) of its weight pressing down on the brain stem.

Your brain is well-protected against small bumps and knocks, but a major impact could cause brain damage. It might make a fragment of skull puncture the meninges and tear brain tissue. That's why wearing a helmet when cycling or skateboarding is such a good idea.

3-second sum-up

Your skull, meninges, and cerebrospinal fluid protect your brain.

3-minute mission Egg head

You need: • 2 fresh eggs • 2 watertight plastic containers with lids • Water

1 Imagine each egg is a brain. Place an egg in each container and fill one with water. Seal both containers with the lids.

2 Drop the containers on the ground from the same height to give them a big bump. One egg may end up scrambled, but the other one should be fine. Which one survives and why?

Answer on page 96.

Your brain is protected by many layers to prevent damage.

Two outer meninges form a barrier between the cranium and the cerebrospinal fluid.

Cerebrospinal fluid

Inner meninges

The brain

The dome-shaped cranium is made of hard, bony plates that join in some places.

Good thinking! Wearing a crash helmet can save your brain so that you can train and play another day.

Parts of the brain
... in 30 seconds

Your brain begins as a tiny tube made of a handful of cells, but undergoes a massive growth spurt as you develop in the womb. By the time you can read this book, your brain boasts billions of cells and is a highly complex organ. Here are some of its major parts:

The cerebrum is the biggest portion of your brain. It's where all your memories are stored and your thoughts and actions are controlled. It has a wrinkly surface called the cerebral cortex. If all its folds and wrinkles were smoothed out, the cortex would measure around 5 ft by 5 ft (about 1.5 m by 1.5 m)—the size of a small picnic blanket. These folds allow more brain material to fit inside the skull, giving humans far more processing power than many other creatures.

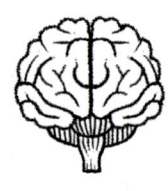

The cerebellum is sometimes called the "little brain." Among its many duties, it helps you figure out distances from objects and also controls and coordinates your balance and movements. Without it, if you tried to stand up, you'd fall over. Ouch!

In front of the cerebellum is the thalamus, your brain's main traffic controller. It filters and directs much of the information coming from the body and senses to different parts of the brain.

3-second sum-up

Your brain is divided into many parts—the largest is the cerebrum.

Brain stem

Apart from linking your brain to the rest of your body through the nervous system, the brain stem performs heroic work every day. It is constantly keeping you alive by controlling many body functions you take for granted, such as breathing, heartbeat, digestion, and blood pressure.

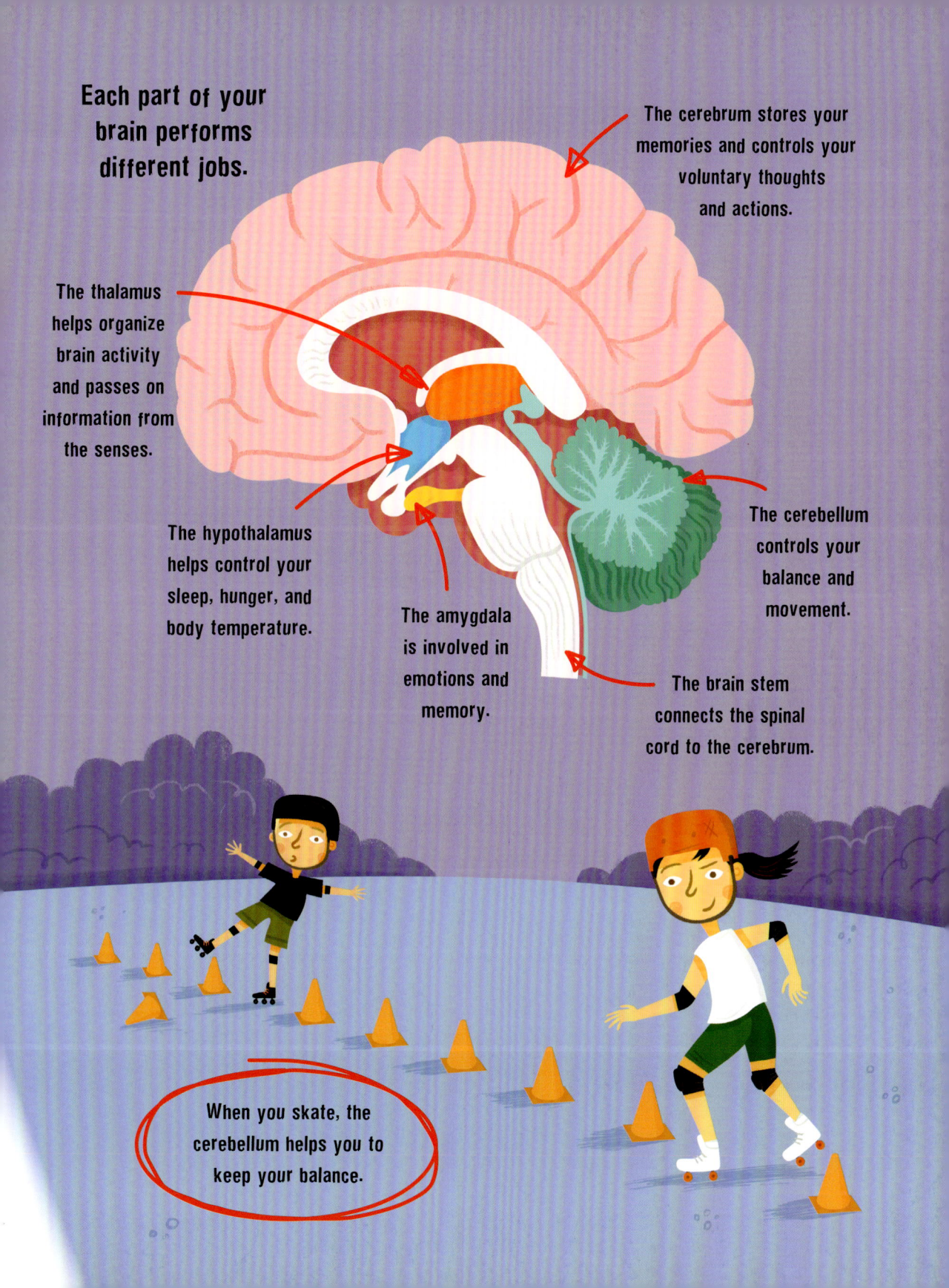

Each part of your brain performs different jobs.

The cerebrum stores your memories and controls your voluntary thoughts and actions.

The thalamus helps organize brain activity and passes on information from the senses.

The hypothalamus helps control your sleep, hunger, and body temperature.

The amygdala is involved in emotions and memory.

The cerebellum controls your balance and movement.

The brain stem connects the spinal cord to the cerebrum.

When you skate, the cerebellum helps you to keep your balance.

Lots of lobes
... in 30 seconds

Scientists divide the cerebrum into four areas known as lobes. While these lobes often work together, each of them also has its own special tasks.

The frontal lobe is where your deep thinking is done. It is responsible for analyzing, thinking ahead, and problem solving, as well as planning your voluntary movements, such as picking up a pen.

The temporal lobe handles your sense of hearing and is involved in the formation of memories. It helps you to recognize and remember sounds and other experiences, and it also allows you to understand speech.

The parietal lobe is hard at work processing all the information from your sense of touch, as well as the positions of your body's joints and muscles. It also helps you pay attention, so that you can listen to your mom or dad while ignoring the chatter of the rest of your family. At the back of your brain, the occipital lobe is your brain's main vision center. Among its many jobs are identifying colors and movement and recognizing objects.

3-second sum-up

The four lobes of the cerebrum are responsible for different tasks.

3-minute mission Lobe one out

Practice learning where each lobe is with a group of friends.

1 One person is the referee. They call out the name of a lobe.

2 The players touch their heads where the lobe is.

3 The referee decides who was last—they are out. Continue play until there's one person left—the winner!

Each of the four lobes in the brain performs a different function.

The parietal lobe lets you know where the parts of your body are and helps you pay attention to your environment.

The frontal lobe allows you to solve problems and think ahead, and helps to form your emotions.

The temporal lobe is involved in processing sounds and memories.

The occipital lobe handles huge amounts of visual information sent by your eyes.

Brain hemispheres
... in 30 seconds

Your brain has two halves, each called a hemisphere. The left and right hemispheres are joined together by a thick bundle of nerves called the corpus callosum. Billions of signals pass between the two hemispheres each day.

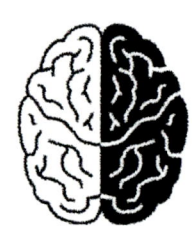

Both hemispheres are similar. They each have four lobes. But they are not identical. The ability to speak and understand language, for example, is controlled by parts of the left hemisphere in most people.

The truly odd thing about the two halves of your brain is that each controls the other side of your body. So when you kick a soccer ball with your right foot, it's your left hemisphere that controls your leg's actions.

Most people have a dominant side. About 90 percent of people are right-handed, while about 70 percent have a dominant right eye. Some people have a mix of dominant body parts, so they may prefer the left hand when writing, but favor the right eye when looking through a telescope.

3-second sum-up
Your brain has left and right halves, each of which controls the body's other side.

3-minute mission Dominant side test

You need: • Tube to look through (e.g. kitchen roll) • Coin

Ask a friend to look through the tube at the coin on the ground, then to put down the tube and step on the coin with one foot, and finally to pick up the coin. Note whether they use their right or left eye, foot, and hand to perform these three tasks. Was one side favored for every task?

Each side, or hemisphere, of the brain sends signals to the opposite side of the body.

Found below the cerebrum, the corpus callosum links both hemispheres and allows them to work together on many tasks.

The left hemisphere of the brain sends a signal to the right foot to move.

The right hemisphere of the brain sends a signal for the left arm to move.

Imaging the brain
... in 30 seconds

Scientists have studied the brain for centuries. Some even used to cut open dead people's heads to take a look inside. Today, scientists usually use less gruesome methods. There are amazing imaging machines that can peer inside living brains and create pictures of them.

A **Computerized Tomography (CT)** scanner takes many X-rays of the brain from all angles. A computer processes these images to build up a detailed picture of the brain, slice by slice. The images can then be turned into a three-dimensional (3D) model of the brain.

An **MRI (Magnetic Resonance Imaging)** scanner uses giant electromagnets. These can help detect the flow of blood around the brain. When one part of the brain is more active, it needs more oxygen, so more blood flows to it. Locating an increase in blood flow using an MRI allows scientists and doctors to detect brain activity in detail. It allows scientists to map the brain and find out which parts do what.

Another way of measuring brain activity is an **EEG**, short for electroencephalogram ... whew! An EEG machine measures the patterns of electrical activity in the brain.

3-second sum-up

Different machines can image the brain and measure what kind of activity is occurring and where.

The 10 percent myth

Some people believe we only use 10 percent of our brains. They're wrong! MRIs and other brain scans have shown how we use almost all parts of our brains at different times. EEG scans have shown that electrical activity from the brain never stops, even when we're asleep.

Machines such as MRI scanners can detect activity inside the brain.

An MRI scanner is shaped like a giant doughnut. It surrounds a person's head and body.

The MRI's electromagnets can weigh 2,200 lb (1,000 kg)—more than most cars.

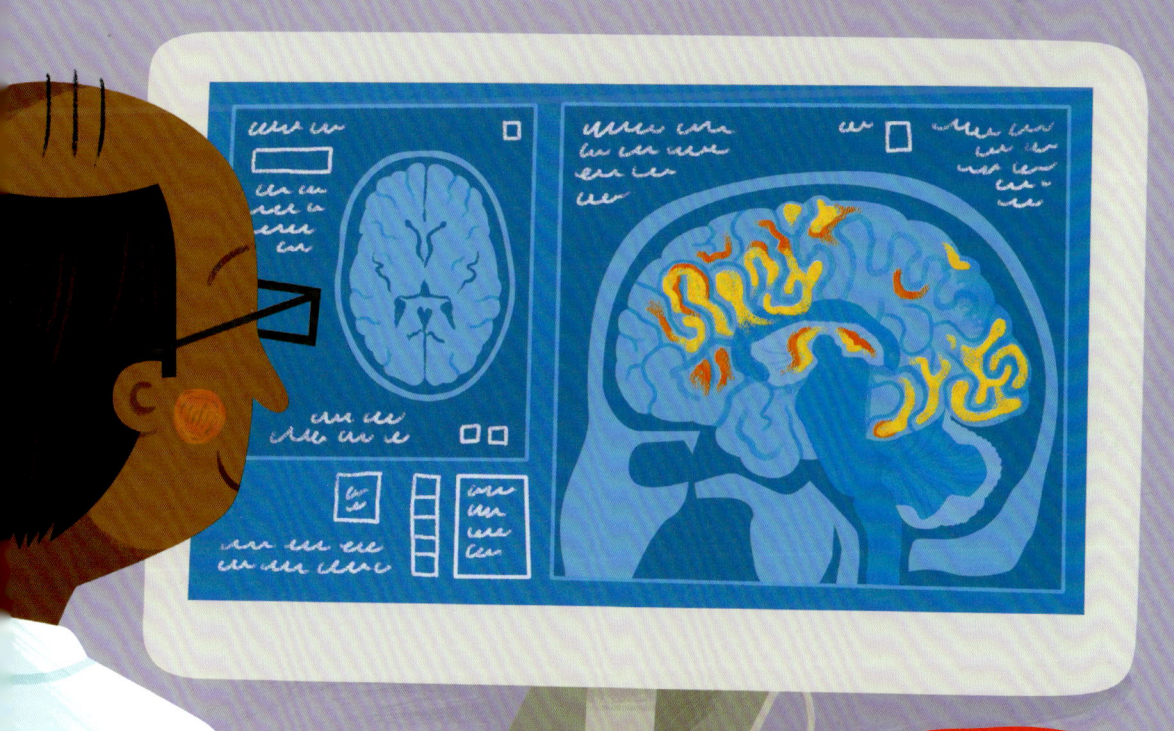

The scanner can detect which parts of the brain are most active when a person is doing a particular task.

The hungry brain

... in 30 seconds

Your brain is seriously busy—so much so, that it generates enough activity to power a 12-watt lightbulb. All that thinking and hard work uses energy. Your brain only weighs about one-fiftieth of your total weight, but it gobbles up one-fifth of the energy your body makes.

Energy is supplied to the brain in the form of glucose, a sugar made by breaking down foods in the digestive system. Glucose, along with oxygen (which is needed to release energy from food), is carried to the brain in blood, which travels through tubes called blood vessels. Blood is pumped through these vessels by your heart.

When you are not at your best, neither is your brain. A lack of sleep or water can affect it. If the glucose or oxygen in the blood dips by a significant amount, your brain may not have the energy it needs to perform well. This can lead to problems with planning, making decisions, and coordinating your body. If your brain is totally starved of either oxygen or glucose for ten minutes or longer, brain damage can occur.

3-second sum-up

The brain is constantly working and uses one-fifth of the body's energy supplies.

3-minute mission Energy levels

See how energy levels can affect a part of your brain's performance.

1 Open a dictionary and read the first 20 entries. Close it.

2 Count to 30. Write down all the words you remember.

Try this in the morning when you feel fresh, and again in the evening when you are tired. When did you perform better?

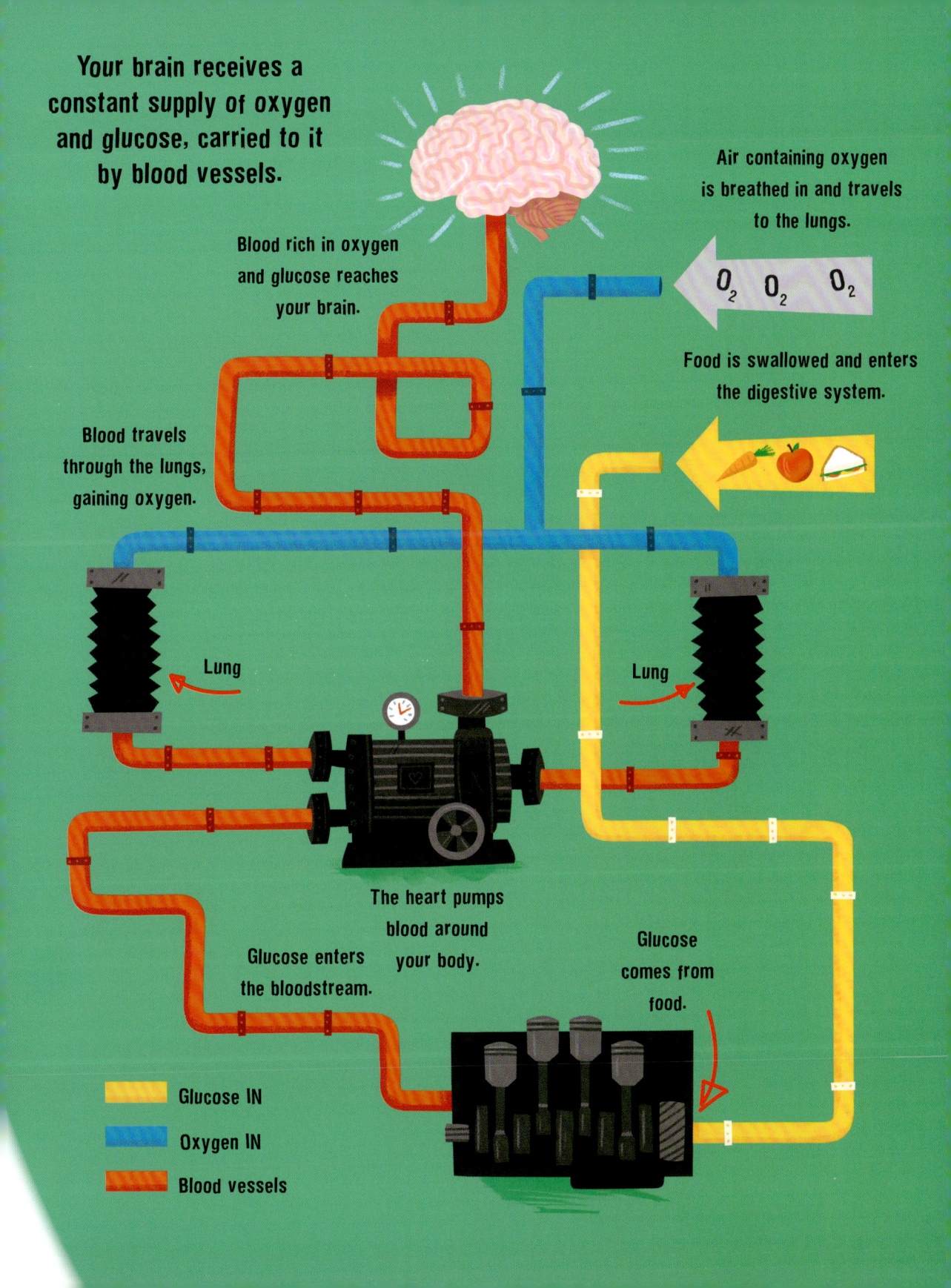

Your brain receives a constant supply of oxygen and glucose, carried to it by blood vessels.

Blood rich in oxygen and glucose reaches your brain.

Air containing oxygen is breathed in and travels to the lungs.

O₂ O₂ O₂

Food is swallowed and enters the digestive system.

Blood travels through the lungs, gaining oxygen.

Lung

Lung

The heart pumps blood around your body.

Glucose enters the bloodstream.

Glucose comes from food.

- Glucose IN
- Oxygen IN
- Blood vessels

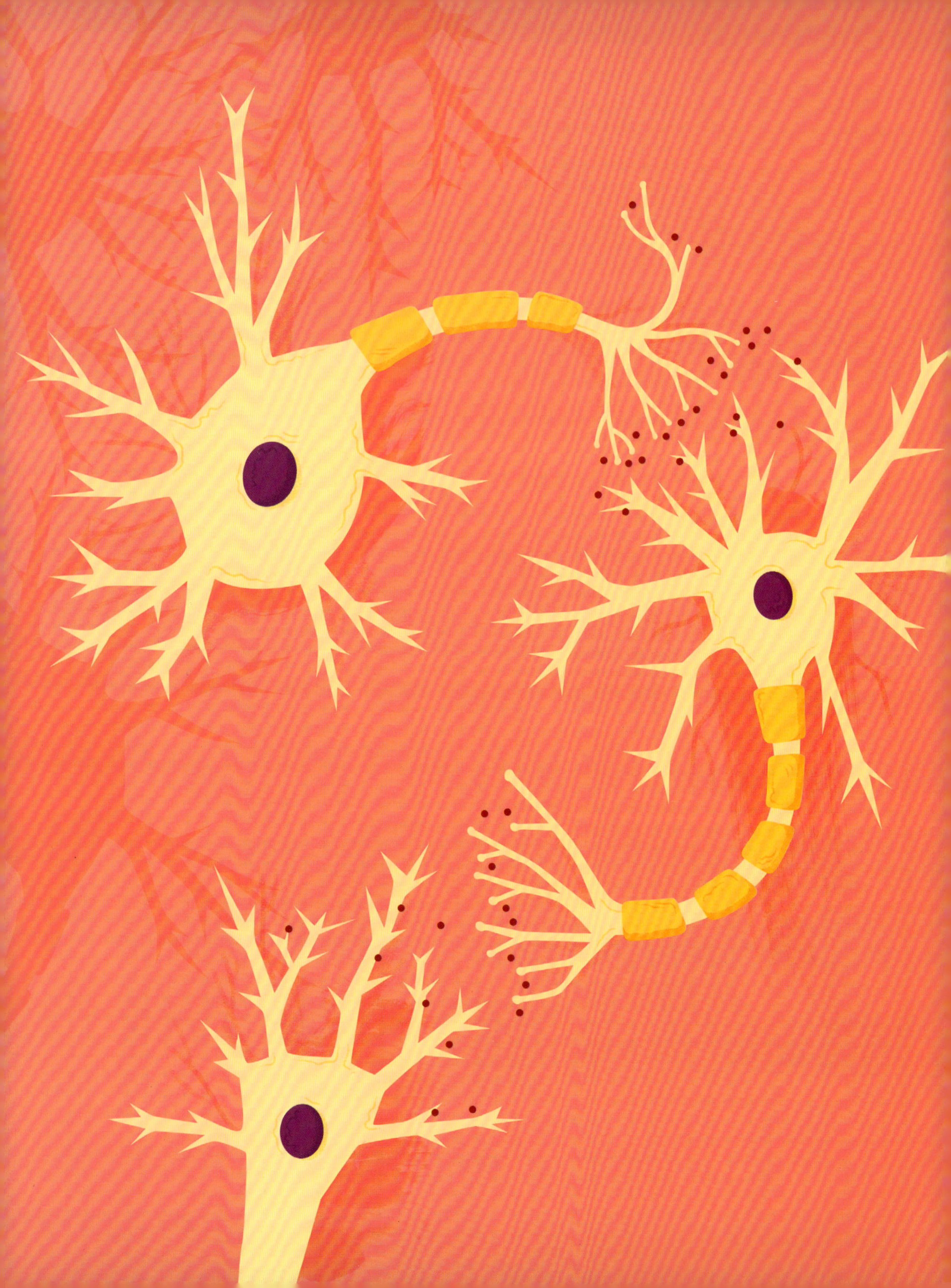

Getting connected

Your brain is incredibly chatty. Not only do all its parts natter away, staying in constant contact with each other, but it also bosses your body around every moment of the day. Your brain is highly skilled at receiving communication from all parts of the body and sending instructions back in return. To do this, it uses two different systems—one uses chemicals in the bloodstream and the other uses an incredible network of nerves that carries electric signals.

Getting connected
Glossary

airways The paths through your nose and mouth that air can travel through.

axon The part of a neuron (nerve cell) that carries a nerve signal away from the cell body.

brain stem The lower part of the brain that connects to the spinal cord.

cell One of the tiny units that make up living things. The human body consists of millions and millions of cells of different types.

central nervous system The part of your body's nervous system that contains the brain, brain stem, and spinal cord.

communicate To pass on or share information with others.

dendrites Fingerlike parts of a nerve cell that carry signals toward a nerve cell's body.

endocrine system A system of different glands that produce chemicals called hormones, which help control and maintain many parts of your body.

gland An organ that produces a hormone for use in the body.

hormones Chemicals produced by glands that carry messages to different parts of your body.

muscle A body part made of fibers, which can contract (get shorter) when receiving a nerve signal.

neurons The technical term for a nerve cell. These specialized cells in the body transmit signals in the nervous system.

neurotransmitters Chemicals that act as messengers, helping to relay signals between the nerve cells.

peripheral nervous system The nervous system outside of the brain and spinal cord.

pupil The black circle in the center of the eye, surrounded by the colored iris, which allows light to enter the eye.

reflex An automatic action performed without thinking by part of your body in response to something.

spinal cord A thick bundle of nerve fibers that runs from the base of the brain through the spine, and that allows the brain to control the body.

synapse A small gap between nerve cells across which signals can pass from one nerve cell to another.

Sending signals
... in 30 seconds

The clever, chatty parts of your brain are made up of neurons, also known as nerve cells. They send and receive information as tiny pulses of electricity, which are called nerve signals or impulses. These signals race from neuron to neuron at speeds of up to about 300 miles (480 km) per hour.

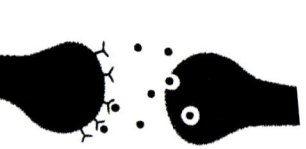

Most neurons are incredibly small. Thousands could fit into a single grain of sand, and your entire brain contains almost 90 billion neurons. In contrast, your pet cat has 760 million and a pond snail just 11,000.

Neurons may be packed together but their ends usually do not touch each other. Instead, there is a small gap between them called a synapse. The electrical nerve signals racing from neuron to neuron need to cross these synapses. They do this with the help of chemicals called neurotransmitters, which stimulate the next nerve cell to carry the signal onward.

3-second sum-up
Huge numbers of nerve cells carry messages around your brain and between your brain and body.

3-minute mission Chain reaction

You need: • Paper • Pen • Large group of people

1 Ask everyone to stand in a row. Each hand is a neuron.

2 Write a message, crumple the paper up into a ball and place it in the end person's hand. That's the nerve signal.

3 On the command "Go," see how fast the message can be passed from hand to hand along the row, with the last person reading the message aloud. Each transfer between hands is a signal jumping a synapse.

Bet you're not as fast as your neurons!

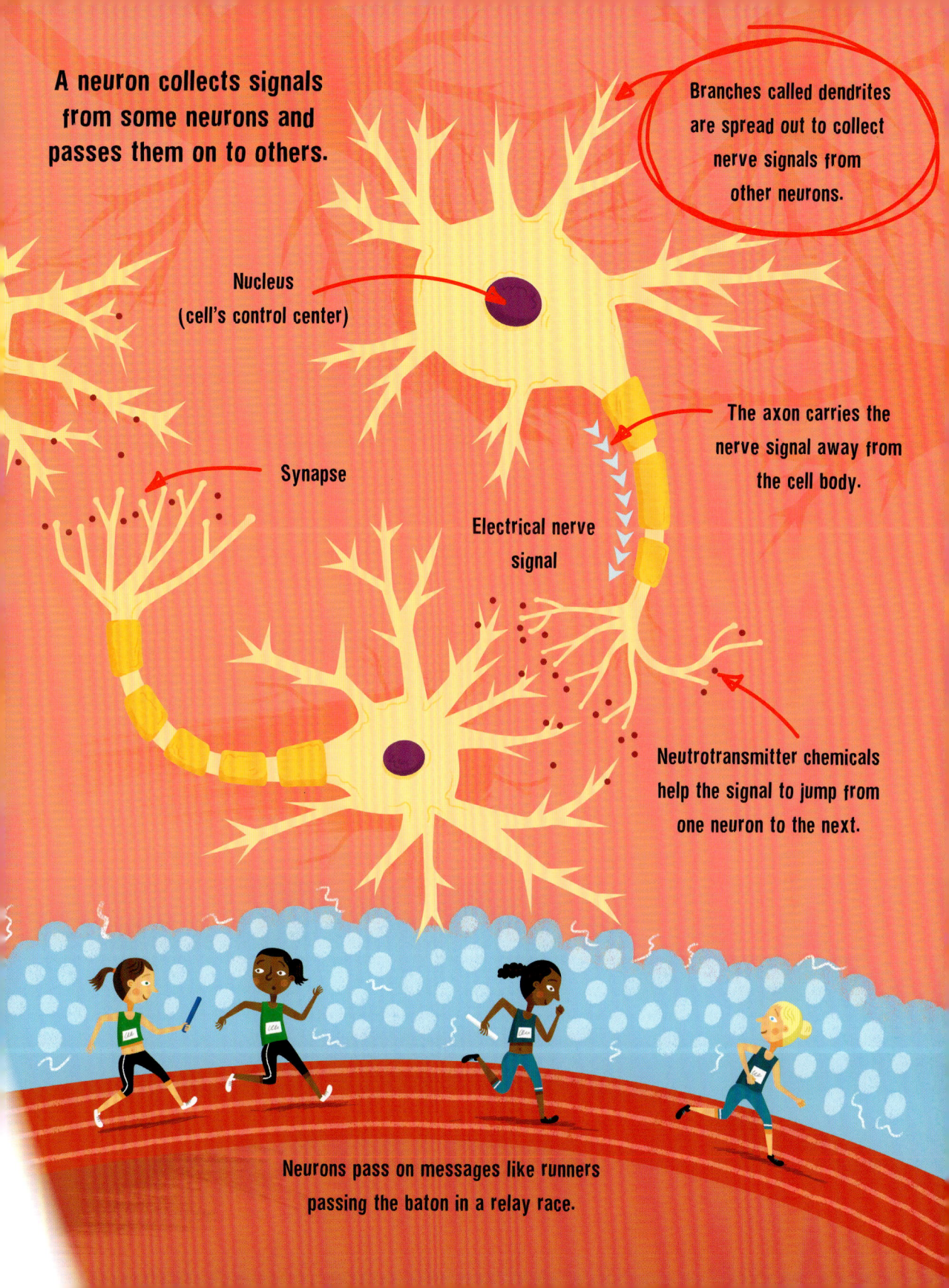

A neuron collects signals from some neurons and passes them on to others.

Branches called dendrites are spread out to collect nerve signals from other neurons.

Nucleus (cell's control center)

Synapse

The axon carries the nerve signal away from the cell body.

Electrical nerve signal

Neutrotransmitter chemicals help the signal to jump from one neuron to the next.

Neurons pass on messages like runners passing the baton in a relay race.

Making connections
... in 30 seconds

Many individual neurons have not one or two but thousands of connections, or links, with others. Together they form an incredibly HUGE network, far more complex than a computer's circuits.

Learning happens when new links are formed in your brain by neurons sharing connections. It may also occur when connections change because you've remembered something or learned a new skill. It's the trillions of links between neurons that make you brainy!

Throughout your life, your brain is constantly rewiring itself. It does this by making new connections and pruning (breaking) old ones. Existing connections also get stronger or weaker. Connections get stronger when more and more signals are repeatedly sent over a connection, such as when you are practicing a new skill. Eventually, you will master the skill and your neurons will rewire, forming and strengthening the connections that make it easier to repeat the skill in the future. Neurons that fire together, wire together!

3-second sum-up

Neurons form trillions of connections in your brain, which are always changing.

Changing brain

Your brain is constantly changing. Before and shortly after you were born, it was growing fast, with as many as 250,000 new neurons forming every minute. As you get older, neurons die off, and the number of connections in your brain decreases. So you are technically brainier than your parents!

There's hope for older people though: learning new skills can help forge new links between neurons and protect against the brain's decline.

To learn a new skill, the brain rewires itself and makes new connections.

Learning a new skill such as juggling can take time as the neurons in your brain form all the necessary links.

The links get stronger the more times signals travel through them. So practice is vital.

Eventually, the links are strong enough that you can repeat the action with ease. Bravo!

Bundle of nerves
... in 30 seconds

Nerve cells are not just found in the brain. They form a large network of nerves that run throughout your entire body. If laid end to end, the nerves outside your brain would stretch 47 miles (75 km).

Nerves are bundles of fibers each made of nerve cells. They vary in size from the smallest, which are finer than a single hair, to the sciatic nerve, which is about ¾ inch (2 cm) in diameter at its widest point.

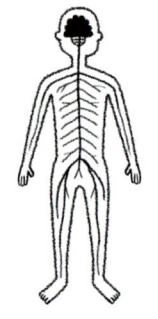

Nerves are like one-way streets. Signals can only travel along a particular nerve in one direction so they cannot bump into signals coming the other way. Sensory nerves send information from the body back to the spinal cord (the bundle of nerves running down your back) and brain. Motor nerves carry instructions from your brain to parts of the body, telling them to move.

Some nerves, such as the optic nerve from your eye, lead straight into your brain. Most, however, are part of your peripheral nervous system. These nerves connect to the spinal cord—your nerve motorway—which speeds information to and from your brain. The spinal cord, brain stem, and brain make up your central nervous system.

3-second sum-up

The brain is linked to the rest of the body via a large network of nerves.

3-minute mission Test your reactions

You need: • Ruler, 12 inches (30 cm) or longer

1 Ask a friend to hold the ruler at the top.

2 Place your thumb and first finger on either side of the bottom of the ruler but not touching it.

3 Ask your friend to drop the ruler without warning. Catch it with your thumb and finger. The shorter the distance, the quicker your reactions. **0–3 inches (0–8 cm): very fast; 6–8 inches (16–21 cm): average; 11 inches (28 cm): slow!**

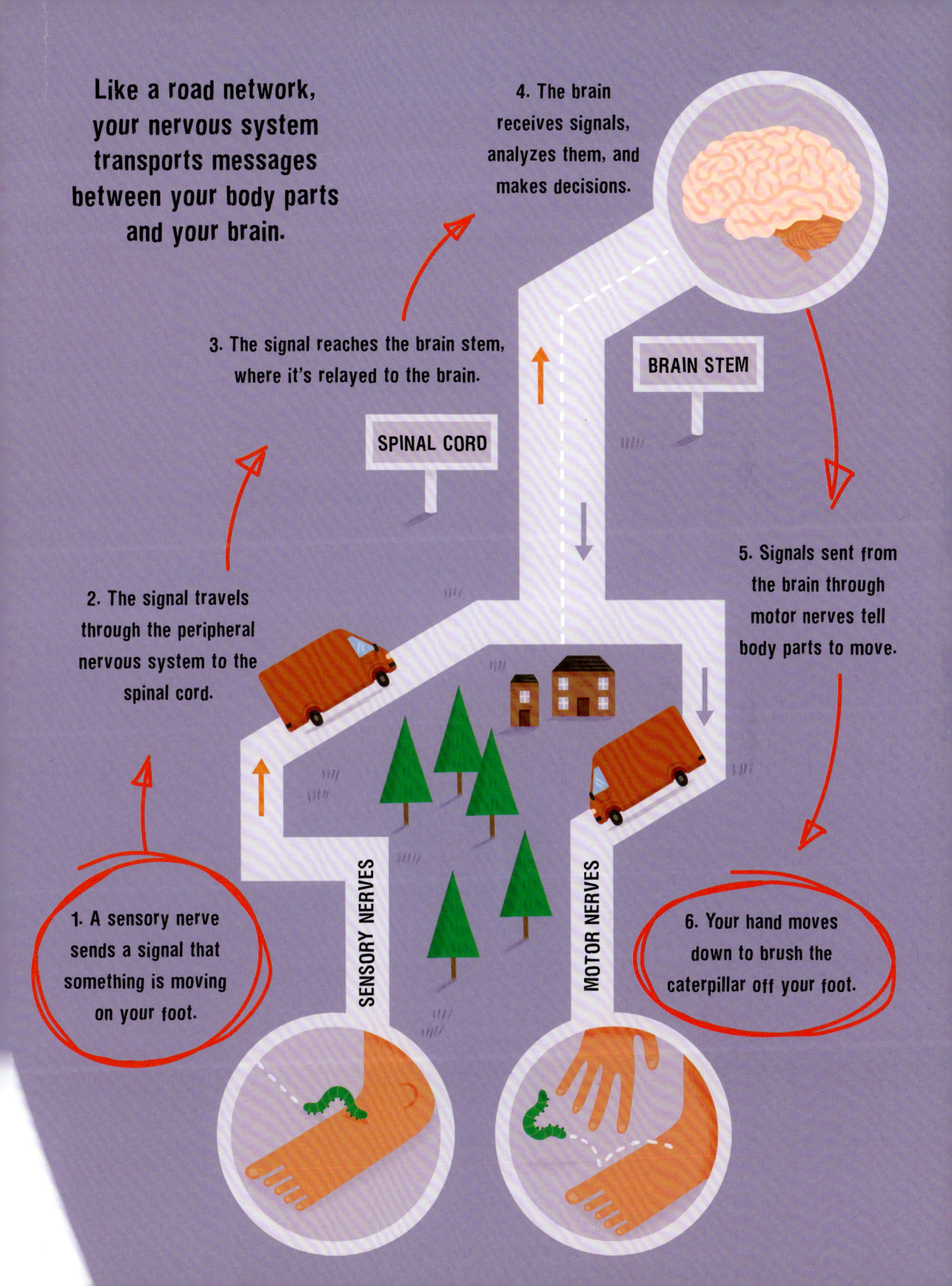

Like a road network, your nervous system transports messages between your body parts and your brain.

4. The brain receives signals, analyzes them, and makes decisions.

3. The signal reaches the brain stem, where it's relayed to the brain.

BRAIN STEM

SPINAL CORD

2. The signal travels through the peripheral nervous system to the spinal cord.

5. Signals sent from the brain through motor nerves tell body parts to move.

SENSORY NERVES

MOTOR NERVES

1. A sensory nerve sends a signal that something is moving on your foot.

6. Your hand moves down to brush the caterpillar off your foot.

Reflexes
... in 30 seconds

For something that weighs as little as a large strawberry—about an ounce (35 grams)—your spinal cord is a marvel. It relays millions of signals to and from your brain and body every second. It's also in charge of a series of rapid reactions that occur without the brain being involved. These are called reflex actions, or reflexes.

Many reflex actions involve nerve signals racing from a part of the body to the spinal cord along a path called a reflex arc. The spinal cord sends a response back. This occurs at a lightning-fast rate—a fraction of a second.

Many reflexes act as a rapid defense system for your body. Have you ever touched a hot cup or sharp broken glass by mistake? Without thinking, your hand jerks away. That's your withdrawal reflex in action, protecting you from continued heat or pain.

Other reflexes include coughing and sneezing, both of which clear your airways of dust, mucus, and other things that might irritate them.

3-second sum-up
Reflexes are automatic reactions that often protect your body.

3-minute mission Shrinking pupils

Dim the lights in a room, count to 50, and look carefully at a friend's pupil—the dark circle in the middle of the eye, which lets light into the back of the eye. Make the lights brighter and check again. Is it bigger or smaller?

Your friend's reflex reaction shrinks the size of the pupil to stop too much bright light from entering and damaging the eye.

Messages are sent via the spinal cord for a quick reaction. This is the reflex arc.

When the skin touches the prickly thorn, it triggers a sensory nerve signal.

The motor nerve signal instructs the muscles in the hand and arm to contract (get shorter).

The signal travels along the reflex arc to the spinal cord.

The hand quickly pulls away from the pain source.

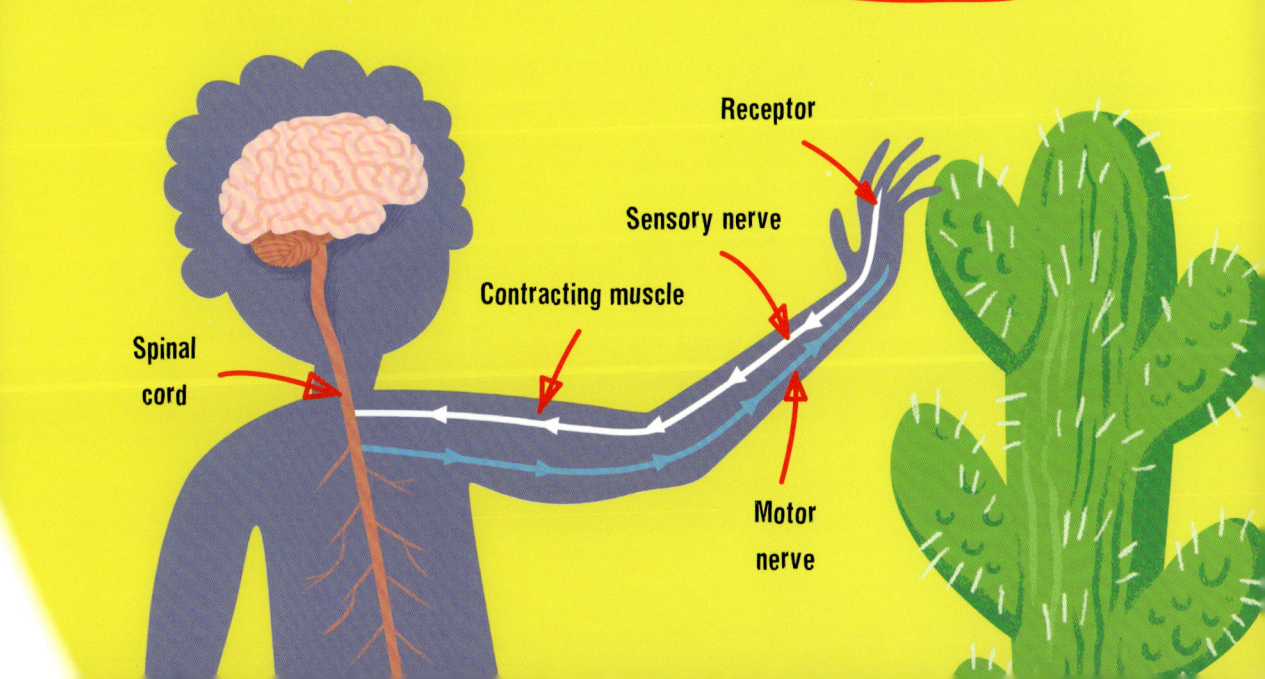

- Receptor
- Sensory nerve
- Contracting muscle
- Spinal cord
- Motor nerve

The endocrine system
... in 30 seconds

The brain has another way of communicating with the body besides the nervous system—through your endocrine system. This system is made up of parts of your body called glands. The endocrine system can prompt chemicals called hormones to be released from the glands and can also sense how these chemicals behave. The pineal gland, for example, produces a hormone called melatonin. This helps control the times when you feel sleepy or wide awake.

Hormones act as chemical messengers. They pass into the bloodstream and are carried around the body to take their messages to particular places. The hormone ADH, for instance, is released by the pituitary gland. It travels round the blood to your kidneys to tell them how much water they should turn into urine.

Perhaps the most important gland in the endocrine system is only the size of a pea and weighs just 0.02 oz (half a gram). The pituitary gland produces hormones that travel to other glands to tell them what to do. It, in turn, communicates with the hypothalamus. This part of the brain controls many of your body's systems and helps make sure everything is balanced and working as it should be.

3-second sum-up

Hormones are chemical messengers that help to control your body.

The bow-tie gland

The thyroid lies across your windpipe and looks a little like a bow tie. It can release a number of hormones, which help make your body's cells work harder and use up energy at a faster rate.

The endocrine system sends messages between your brain and body using glands and the hormones they produce.

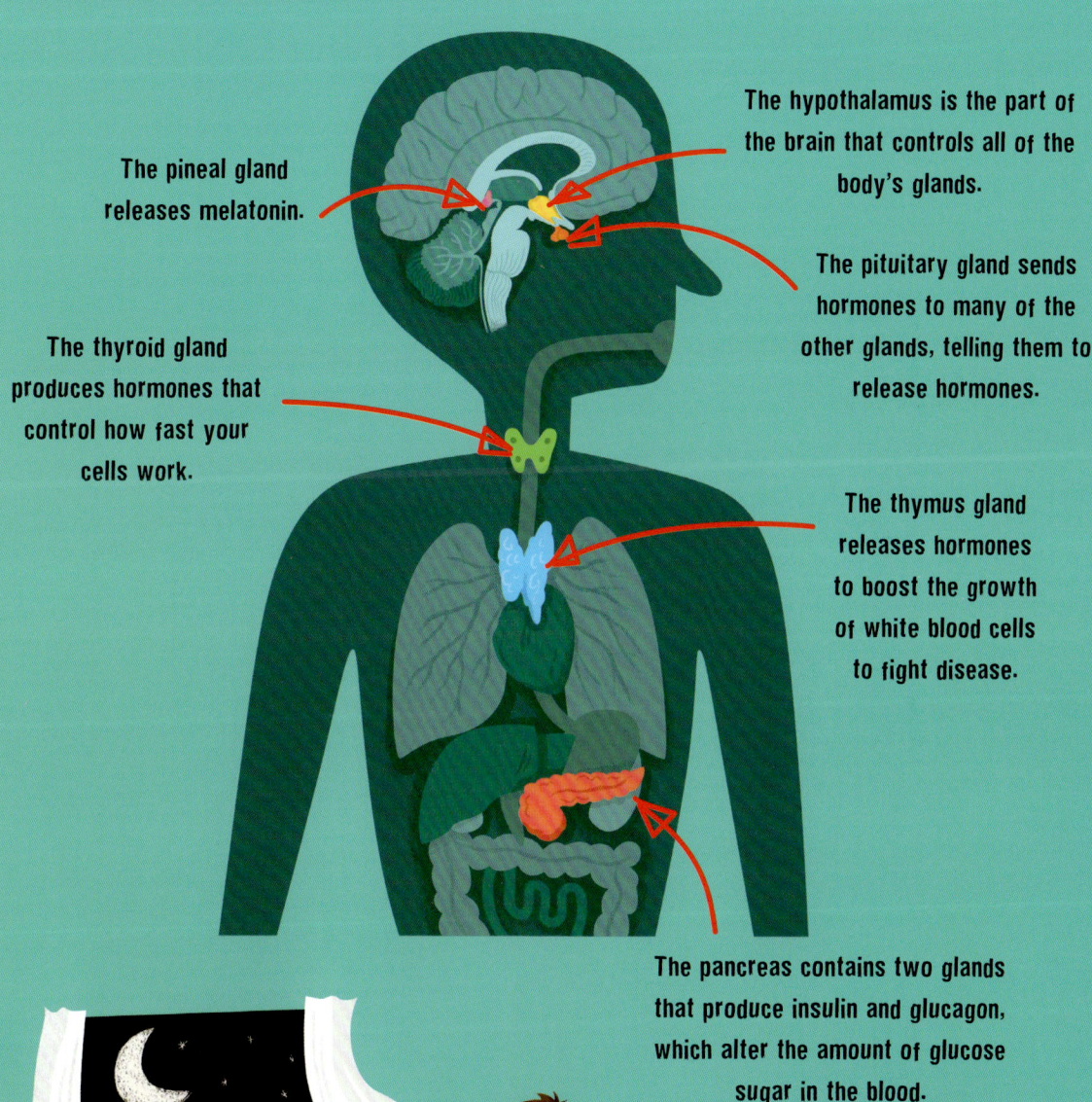

The pineal gland releases melatonin.

The hypothalamus is the part of the brain that controls all of the body's glands.

The pituitary gland sends hormones to many of the other glands, telling them to release hormones.

The thyroid gland produces hormones that control how fast your cells work.

The thymus gland releases hormones to boost the growth of white blood cells to fight disease.

The pancreas contains two glands that produce insulin and glucagon, which alter the amount of glucose sugar in the blood.

Melatonin helps the body know when it is time to go to sleep.

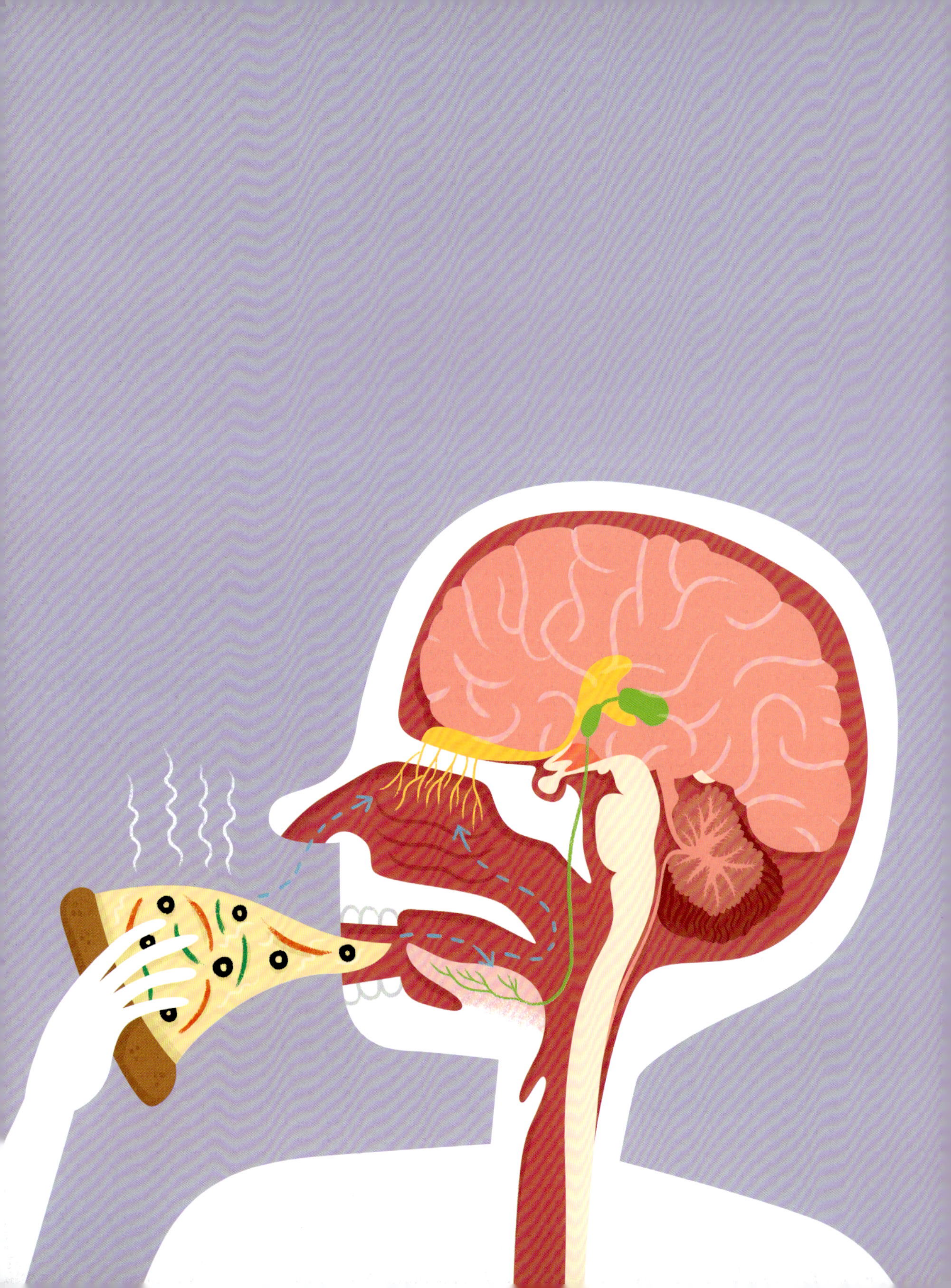

Making sense

Your brain may be incredibly powerful, but without your senses it would be deaf, blind, and dumb! Your body's senses provide your brain with absolutely crucial information about the outside world and your place in it. Without senses, you would not be able to experience and learn all the things you do or create memories of events that have happened in the past. Your major senses are sight, hearing, smell, taste, and touch but you have other senses as well.

Making sense
Glossary

binaural hearing The sense of hearing experienced with two ears.

cochlea A coiled tube in your inner ear that is filled with liquid and helps to convert sound vibrations into electrical nerve signals.

focus The way your eyes look at an image to make it clear and sharp.

molecule Two or more tiny particles called atoms, chemically joined together.

occipital lobe The lobe at the back of the brain that handles information sent by the eyes.

odorant A tiny particle of a substance that gives it its smell and can be sensed by the nerve cells in your nose.

olfactory bulb A bulb-shaped part of the brain that receives signals about smells from the nerve cells inside the nose.

perception How the brain interprets and makes sense of the information sent to it by all of your senses.

proprioception The sense of knowing the position, location, and movement of the body and its parts.

pupil The black circle in the center of your eye, surrounded by the colored iris, which allows light to enter the eye.

retina Part of the back of the eye, which is packed with light-sensitive nerve cells that turn light into electrical signals.

thalamus Part of the brain that relays signals from the senses to other parts of the brain and connects different parts of the cortex together.

three dimensions (3D) If you can see things in 3D, you can see they have not only height and width but also depth.

vibration A slight shaking movement that makes something wobble or tremble.

Taste and smell
... in 30 seconds

Your incredible sense of smell can detect many millions of different scents—from a stinky sports sock to the delightful aroma of a freshly baked pizza.

Smell relies on a patch inside each nostril no bigger than a postage stamp. Each patch contains millions of tiny hairs called cilia. These capture odorants—tiny molecules in the air that cause smell—and prompt signals in the two olfactory bulbs in the brain.

Smell has its own connection straight to the brain via the olfactory bulbs. Unlike other senses, these signals are processed by the same side of the brain. So if you sniff something with only your left nostril, the left side of your brain does the processing.

Smell also helps your sense of taste. You have several thousand taste buds on your tongue and the cheeks and roof of your mouth. These send signals to the gustatory cortex, allowing you to detect five basic tastes—sweet, sour, bitter, salty, and umami (a savory taste found in meat and cheese). Your brain combines the taste and smell to figure out the food's flavor. That's why food seems tasteless when you have a cold and your nose is blocked.

3-second sum-up

Taste buds and olfactory bulbs send signals to the brain about flavors and smells.

3-minute mission Smell the flavor

You need: Two foods with a similar texture, such as a slice of pear and a slice of apple, or different flavors of jelly beans.

Your nose helps to figure out the flavor of food. To demonstrate this, blindfold a friend and ask them to hold their nose. Give them two similar foods to taste. Can they tell which is which? Now allow them to use their nose. What difference does it make to the test? It should make it easier to get the right answer.

Your brain uses smell and taste to figure out the flavor of food.

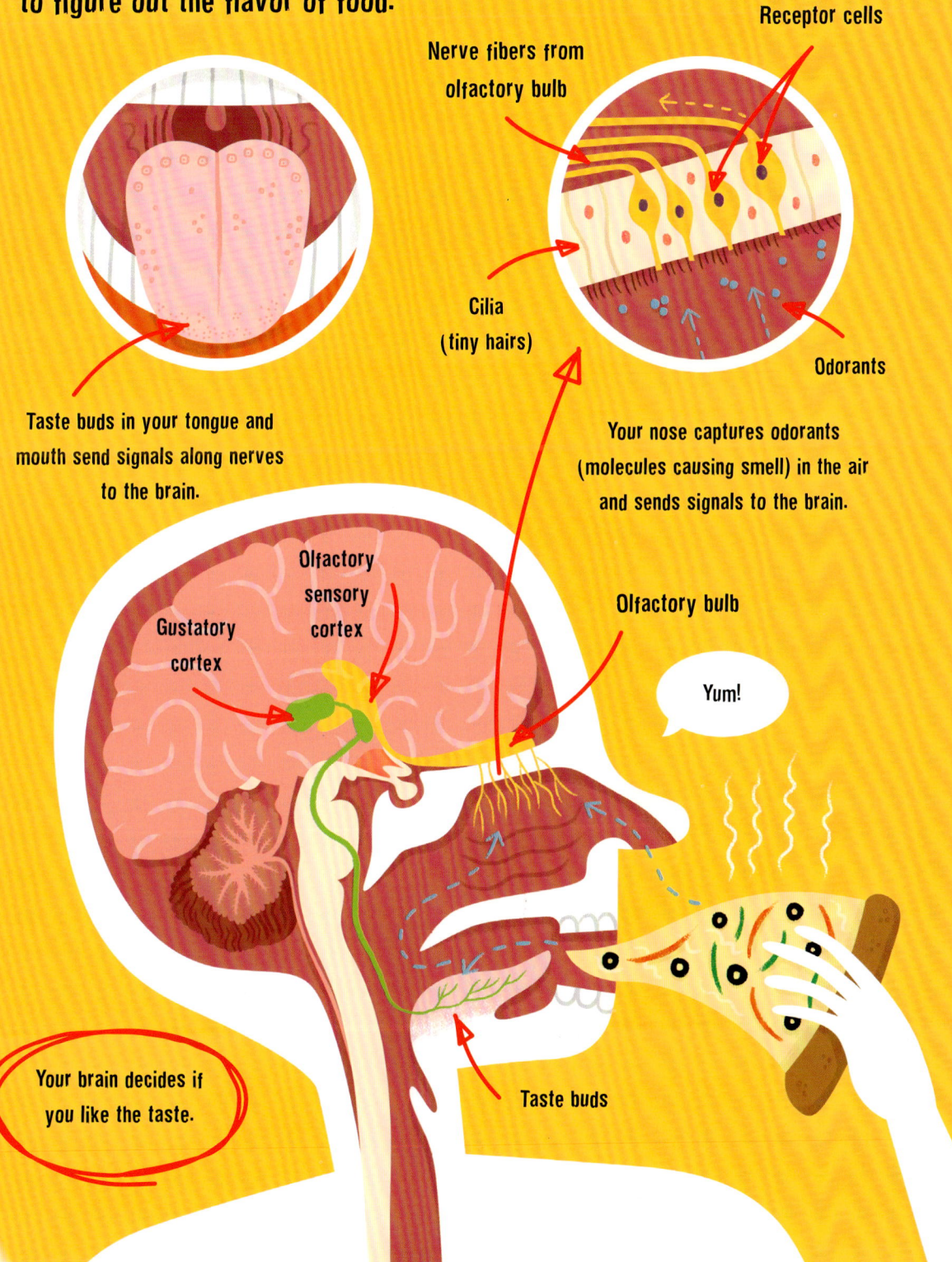

Receptor cells

Nerve fibers from olfactory bulb

Cilia (tiny hairs)

Odorants

Taste buds in your tongue and mouth send signals along nerves to the brain.

Your nose captures odorants (molecules causing smell) in the air and sends signals to the brain.

Gustatory cortex

Olfactory sensory cortex

Olfactory bulb

Yum!

Taste buds

Your brain decides if you like the taste.

Hearing
... in 30 seconds

Sounds start as vibrations traveling as waves through the air. Your sense of hearing allows you to detect and identify millions of different sounds, from a strummed guitar to someone calling your name.

Those big flappy ears perched on your head are only part of the story. Most of the hard work is performed inside your skull. There, sounds vibrate a small eardrum. The vibrations are made stronger by three tiny bones, one of which—the stapes—is the smallest bone in your body: 3/32 by 1/8 inch (2.5 x 3 mm).

The vibrations enter a snail-shaped structure called the cochlea, where they move tiny hairs that turn them into electrical signals. These signals are sent by nerves to your brain to make sense of the sounds and to recognize them from memory.

Your two ears give you binaural hearing. They enable your brain to figure out where a sound comes from. The ear nearest the sound detects it first and sends signals to the brain a fraction of a second before the other ear.

3-second sum-up

Vibrations gathered by the ear are sent as nerve signals to the brain.

3-minute mission Trick your ears

You need: • 2 plastic funnels or cones made of card • 2 x 12-inch pieces of plastic tube • Tape

1 Tape a tube around the small end of each funnel and gently hold the ends of the tubes to your ears.

2 Cross the funnels over so that they point in opposite directions.

3 Close your eyes. Ask a friend to walk around you and call your name. Point to where you think they are. Were you right? Chances are, your crossed-over hearing got it wrong.

Sounds vibrate in our eardrums, turn into electrical signals, and are sent to the brain to make sense of them.

The auditory nerve carries the signals to the brain.

Three tiny bones called ossicles amplify (increase) the vibrations.

The cochlea turns the vibrations into electrical signals.

Sounds travel down the auditory canal to make the eardrum vibrate.

The outer ear acts like a funnel, gathering in sounds.

When a source of sound is moving, the brain has to continually figure out where it is coming from.

Some sounds, such as dog whistles, are too high-pitched for humans to hear.

Sight
... in 30 seconds

Two small, bulging balls filled with jelly work with your brain to give you the amazing sense of sight. These are your eyes.

Your eyes let light travel through a clear protective dome (the cornea), a hole (the pupil), and then a curved lens just ⅓ inch (8.5 mm) in diameter. The lens focuses the light onto the back of the eye, called the retina, which contains over 100 million special nerve cells.

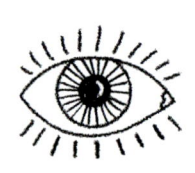

These nerve cells respond to light that reaches them, creating nerve signals. The signals travel along the optic nerve to the thalamus and then the occipital lobes at the back of the brain. There's plenty of work still to be done. The brain has to interpret all the signals, detect colors, and recognize objects to make sense of the information.

Because they are 2 inches (5 cm) apart, each eye sees a scene from a slightly different angle and sends back slightly different streams of information. Your brain uses these differences to help it figure out depth and build a 3D world from the signals it receives.

3-second sum-up
Light enters the eye and causes nerve cells within it to send signals to the brain.

3-minute mission Put a hole in your hand

You need: • Long cardboard tube

1 Hold the tube up to your right eye, then stare with both eyes at a blank wall for 15 seconds.

2 Bring a hand up in front of your left eye. It looks like there's a hole in it! This is because your brain processes your eyes' two views into one image. It ignores much of the dark tube and focuses on the hole at the tube's end, which it then merges with the image of your hand from the left eye.

Light comes in through our eyes, our brain processes the information, and we can see the world.

The brain interprets the signals so that we see the world right-side up.

Light enters the eye and hits the lens.

Ahhh! It's a bear!

The lens focuses the light and it crosses over inside the eye.

The image on the retina is upside down.

Nerve cells on the retina send electrical signals to the brain.

Touch and other senses
... in 30 seconds

Get a grip! Or a stroke, push, or pinch. Whenever your skin comes into contact with objects, your sense of touch is at work. Millions of touch-sensor nerve cells are in your skin, noticing any contact and sending signals through the nervous system to your brain.

These touch sensors are not spread out evenly. Your back and calves only have a handful while your lips and hands are jam-packed with them—there are up to 3,000 for every $1/8$ square inch (about 1 square cm) on your fingertips. These sensors let you feel vibrations, pressure, and textures—from hard beach stones to your hamster's soft fur.

Other special nerve cells in the skin give you even more senses. Thermoreceptors sense hot and cold, while nociceptors detect pain. Your sense of pain protects you from harm by making you aware of danger and telling you that a part of your body is injured and needs attention.

Sensor cells in your muscles and joints measure how much your muscles are stretched at one moment as well as the angle of your joints. This information gives you the sense of proprioception—knowing where all your body parts are without looking and checking all the time.

3-second sum-up
Touch sensors in your skin allow you to sense pressure, texture, and vibrations.

3-minute mission Proprioception test

1 Hold your arms out, cross them, and put your palms together.

2 Interlock your fingers and turn your hands up between your arms so you're looking at your knuckles.

3 Ask someone to point to one of your index fingers. Try to move it. You might move the wrong finger because your brain struggles to combine proprioception and vision signals to identify which finger belongs to which hand.

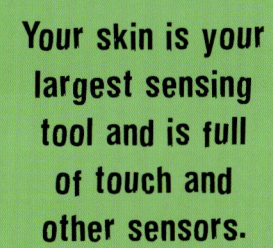

Your skin is your largest sensing tool and is full of touch and other sensors.

Epidermis—outer layer of skin

This thermoreceptor senses cold. Others sense heat.

Nociceptor (pain receptor)

Touch receptor

Pressure receptor

A cross-section of your skin shows the receptors.

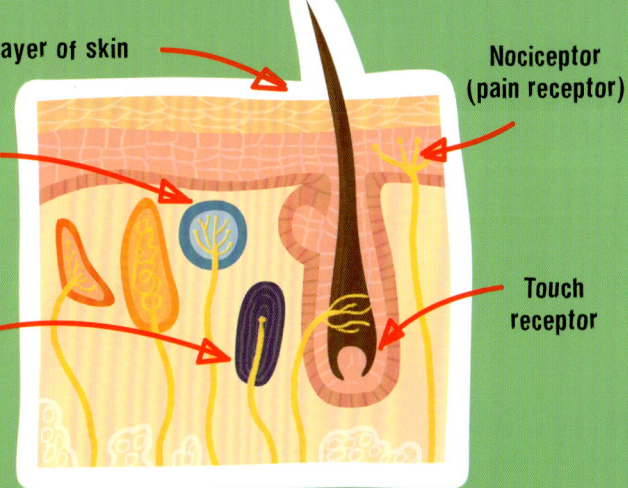

Touch sensors detect the difference between a heavy weight pressing down and the light touch of a balloon.

Ouch!

Thermoreceptors send signals to the brain when they detect something cold or hot.

Your lips sense the texture of food they touch.

Nociceptors sense pain and make you move away from its source.

Perception
... in 30 seconds

You don't just see with your eyes, you see with your brain! The signals your eyes send to the brain are like parts of a puzzle. Your brain pieces together all the signals and information to decide what they all mean. And it does this for all of your senses, not just sight.

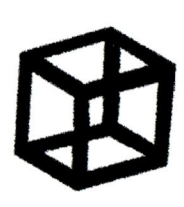

Your brain seeks out ways to interpret and understand all of the information sent to it, using many different rules. These include size constancy—the idea that the same object appears smaller when it is farther away and bigger when it is nearby.

Amazingly, your brain is an extremely good guesser. Most of its best guesses are correct or nearly right, but sometimes, as in the case of optical illusions, your brain gets it wrong.

Perceptions formed from information sent by one sense can influence another. One scientific study showed that when red food dye (which had no flavor) was added to a clear soft drink, children described the red drink as tasting more fruity than the clear drink—even though they were exactly the same!

3-second sum-up

Perceptions are your brain's best explanation of the information sent to it by your senses.

3-minute mission Test your brain

Optical illusions meddle with your brain's abilities to make best guesses about the information it receives from your eyes. They help show the shortcuts and rules the brain uses to make these guesses. Test your own brain with the optical illusions opposite.

Answers on page 96.

Optical illusions can trick your brain into seeing things differently from how they really are.

1. What creature do you see?

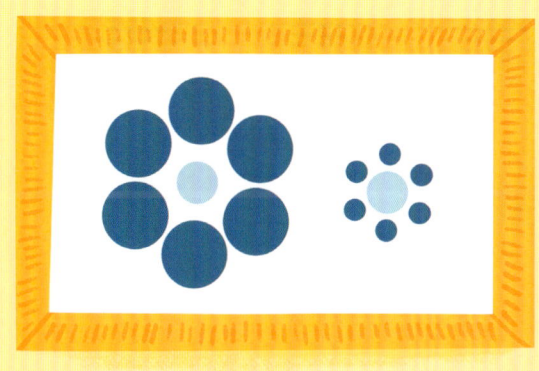

2. Which center circle is largest?

3. Are the diagonal lines parallel or not?

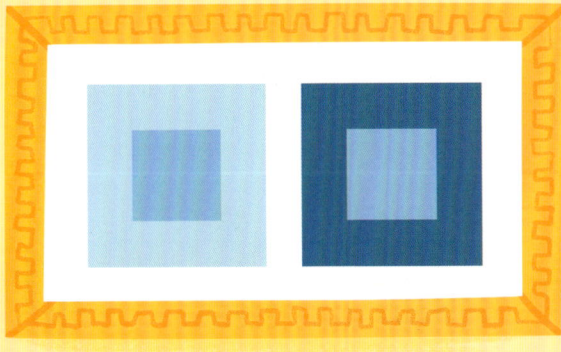

4. Which center square is brighter and lighter?

Taking shortcuts
... in 30 seconds

That poor, busy brain of yours is working overtime, making its best guesses as it's bombarded with information. You can hardly blame it for taking shortcuts and looking for the simplest explanation for the information it receives.

Your brain likes patterns because these can help it quickly make sense of complicated scenes. It also likes to group things together that are either similar, such as similar-colored dots, or close to each other, such as the sounds that form a phone ringtone, as it figures things out.

And that's not all. Your brain can be a bit like an annoying friend who cannot help finishing the ends of your sentences. It constantly fills in gaps in the information it receives, such as mentally filling in the rest of a dog or cat when all you can see is the front half peeking around a corner.

You can test your brain's habit of seeing patterns and filling in shapes. For instance, some optical illusions trick the brain into seeing the edge and shapes of objects that aren't there. These are known as illusory contours.

3-second sum-up

The brain makes shortcuts as it seeks out simple solutions to the information it's sent.

Pareidolia

Sometimes, your brain is over-enthusiastic about finding patterns. When it detects patterns or connections between pieces of information where none truly exist, it is known as pareidolia. For example, some people see human faces in all sorts of things—rocks, clouds in the sky, or on the surface of a piece of toast.

Your brain tries to fill in gaps in visual information to make sense of what it sees.

Your brain quickly perceives a complete image of a tiger on the prowl even though parts of the image are missing.

Your brain sees these shapes as spikes sticking out of a ball. But there is no ball. This is an illusory contour image.

This arrangement of circles and white flat squares gives the impression of a pyramid inside, even though there isn't one.

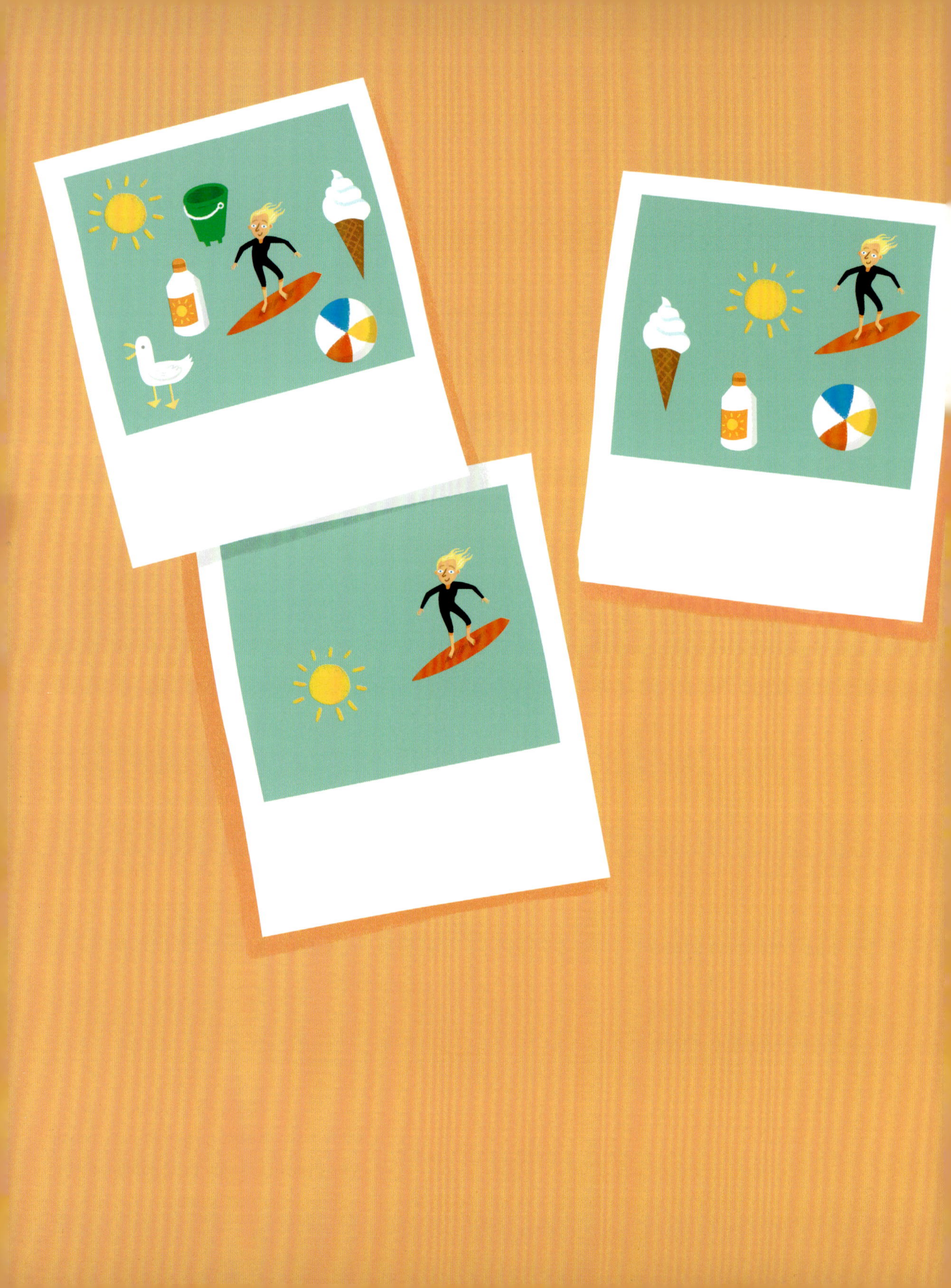

Memory

What's your name? Where do you live? Who are your best friends? What is the capital of Italy? The answers to these and thousands more facts—both important and trivial—are all held in your memory. Without it, you wouldn't know who you are or any facts about the world. Memory gives you the ability to store and retrieve thoughts, experiences, and facts. It comes in different types and can be improved a little using certain techniques.

Memory Glossary

acronym A word formed from the first letter or letters of a series of words, for example, UFO = Unidentified Flying Object.

association A feeling, memory, or thought linked with other thoughts or a person, place, or object.

chunking A helpful memory technique where you split up long pieces of information into smaller, easy-to-remember chunks.

encoded When information is converted into a different form; for example, for storage in long-term memory.

long-term memory A type of memory that can hold possibly unlimited numbers of facts or experiences for a long time.

mnemonic (say: nemonic) A memory aid such as a rhyme or verse that helps you to remember a series of facts.

recall To be able to remember something you have learned or something that happened in the past.

recognition Being able to match something you see to something in your memory.

retrieval The way in which information is recalled from your memory.

sensory memory A type of memory used to hold information from your senses, which lasts less than half a second.

short-term memory A type of memory that lasts about half a minute and can only hold about five to nine items.

Making memories
... in 30 seconds

Sensory memory is the shortest and fastest memory type. It holds information gathered by your senses such as a sound, a visual scene, or the sensation that your finger has touched something soft. It usually lasts less than half a second.

If something held in your sensory memory interests your brain, it will focus attention on it and pass it to your short-term memory. This stores things such as the first part of a math problem while you read the rest of it. Without short-term memory, you'd be lost. By the time you'd read the end of this sentence, you'd have forgotten how it started!

Your short-term memory can hold around five to nine items for 20 to 30 seconds. If your brain doesn't pay attention to an item during this time, it slips out of memory and is forgotten. If your brain focuses on an item in its short-term memory, there's a chance it will pass into long-term memory—your major memory storage system.

3-second sum-up

Different types of memory include sensory, short-term, and long-term.

3-minute mission Short-term memory test

1 Ask two friends to stand in a room. Enter the room and look round for 30 seconds, taking in as much information as you can.

2 Leave the room for one minute. In this time, your friends should make 12 changes, such as changing their position, swapping clothes, or moving objects.

3 Go back in the room. How many changes can you find?

Some information from your senses is transferred to short-term memory, while some of it may go into your long-term memory.

Do you remember that really hot vacation last summer, with the amazing surfer?

Sensory memory

The brain holds sensory information such as sights, sounds, and smells for about half a second.

Short-term memory

Your brain stores some information in short-term memory for 20-30 seconds but the rest is forgotten.

Long-term memory

If you give attention to an item in short-term memory, it may be stored in your long-term memory.

Long-term memory
... in 30 seconds

Your long-term memory is packed with information. As you grow up, it builds to become an awesome store of facts and experiences. Scientists split these up into different types of memories.

Semantic memory is information about the world. It's made up of facts and rules, such as knowing where France is on a map or the rules of soccer. Episodic memory is like your own diary, recording events and memories of your own life. Procedural memory stores information about how to do things—such as tying a knot or swimming backstroke.

Unlike a smartphone's memory card or a computer's hard disk drive, these different memories are not all stored in one place. They are stored all over your brain.

You access your long-term memory many times each day and in different ways. Recognition is when you spot something learned or experienced before, such as a face in a crowd. Recall is when you summon up a memory without any clues from the outside world. It is usually harder than recognition.

3-second sum-up

You store facts, events, and skills in your long-term memory.

3-minute mission Test your powers of recall

Stare at List 1 for 60 seconds. Do something else for 15 minutes. Then write down all of the words you can recall. Repeat with List 2. You probably remembered more of the List 2 words because they are objects and you can see images of them in your mind.

List 1: absent, mood, idea, friendly, secret, good, boring, unknown, valuable, time

List 2: glasses, umbrella, banana, tiger, rocket, phone, dinosaur, envelope, police officer, bee

Every day you access different types of long-term memory.

Knowing that this tree is an oak and that oaks lose their leaves in fall are examples of semantic memory.

Seeing the cold drinks vendor triggers episodic memory about the last time you visited.

Riding a bike makes use of procedural memory of skills.

Unlike this helmet camera that stores images exactly as they're filmed, your memories can change every time you recall something.

Forgetting
... in 30 seconds

Not remembering things can be useful. It allows the brain to store only the most important facts and memories. But occasionally you struggle to remember important things, such as a friend's birthday or the items on a shopping list in your head.

There are many reasons why your memory sometimes lets you down. You may not have been paying full attention at the time the memory was made. This means it has not been encoded and stored accurately in your brain.

Interference can also make you forget things. This happens when some memories compete with others. You might learn a new computer password and forget your old one. Perhaps you've visited a place a number of times but can't remember on which visit you bumped into your best friend.

Some memories are hard to recall because they are not linked well with others. Your brain likes to make links, known as associations, between different pieces of information. Associating something new with something you already know helps embed the new information in your memory.

3-second sum-up

There are several reasons why we remember some things and forget others.

3-minute mission Memory game

1 Play with at least two friends. The first person names one item you might pack for your vacation.

2 The next person repeats the item and adds another one.

3 Continue in this way, repeating all the previous items and adding one more. Try making associations between the items. Does it help you remember them better?

There can be different reasons why you forget details, such as the items on a shopping list.

If you don't pay full attention, information may not be stored correctly in your memory.

Stop playing that video game. Go and buy two cans of tomatoes, six buns, and some sliced ham!

Hi! I'm here to buy sliced cheese, plums, and three cans of beans.

Am I buying two tins of plums, three buns, and sliced ham—or was it cheese?

New memories can interfere with old ones.

Memory aids
... in 30 seconds

As well as using associations to help you remember things, you can use "chunking"—breaking down long bits of information into smaller, bite-sized pieces that are easier to remember.

A long set of numbers found on a bank card can be split up into smaller chunks to aid memory. Chunking can also be used when mastering a new skill. Learning to serve in tennis can be split up into parts, such as the ball toss, moving back the racket, and then swinging it forward.

Did you know the ancient Greeks had a goddess of memory? She was called Mnemosyne and gave her name to a memory aid—mnemonics (say: "nemonics"). These are phrases that help you remember things in the right order, such as Never Eat Slimy Worms for the points of the compass—North, East, South, and West.

Another mnemonic, "My Very Educated Mother Just Served Us Nachos!" helps you remember the order of the planets from the Sun (Mercury, Venus, Earth, Mars, Jupiter, Saturn, Uranus, Neptune). See if you can make up your own memorable mnemonics for remembering short lists of information.

3-second sum-up

Different tips and tricks can help improve your memory.

3-minute mission Build a memory palace

1 Make a memory palace to help you remember the words below. Think of the things in different places at home to make associations. For example, Mount Everest could be the stairs and the octopus could be in the bathtub.

2 The next day, go through the rooms in your head. How many items can you recall?

Zebra, eagle, alligator, lion, skunk, sports car, penguin, banana, Mount Everest, octopus

Techniques like chunking and association help us to recall essential information, such as a long login number.

First break the number down into smaller chunks.

22 68 13

Place each number somewhere memorable in your house.

2 2 68

There are two sets of two windows in my bedroom and a photo of my granddad, who is 68.

Making associations can link new memories to strong, older ones.

2013

The last two digits stand for 2013—the last time my team won the cup.

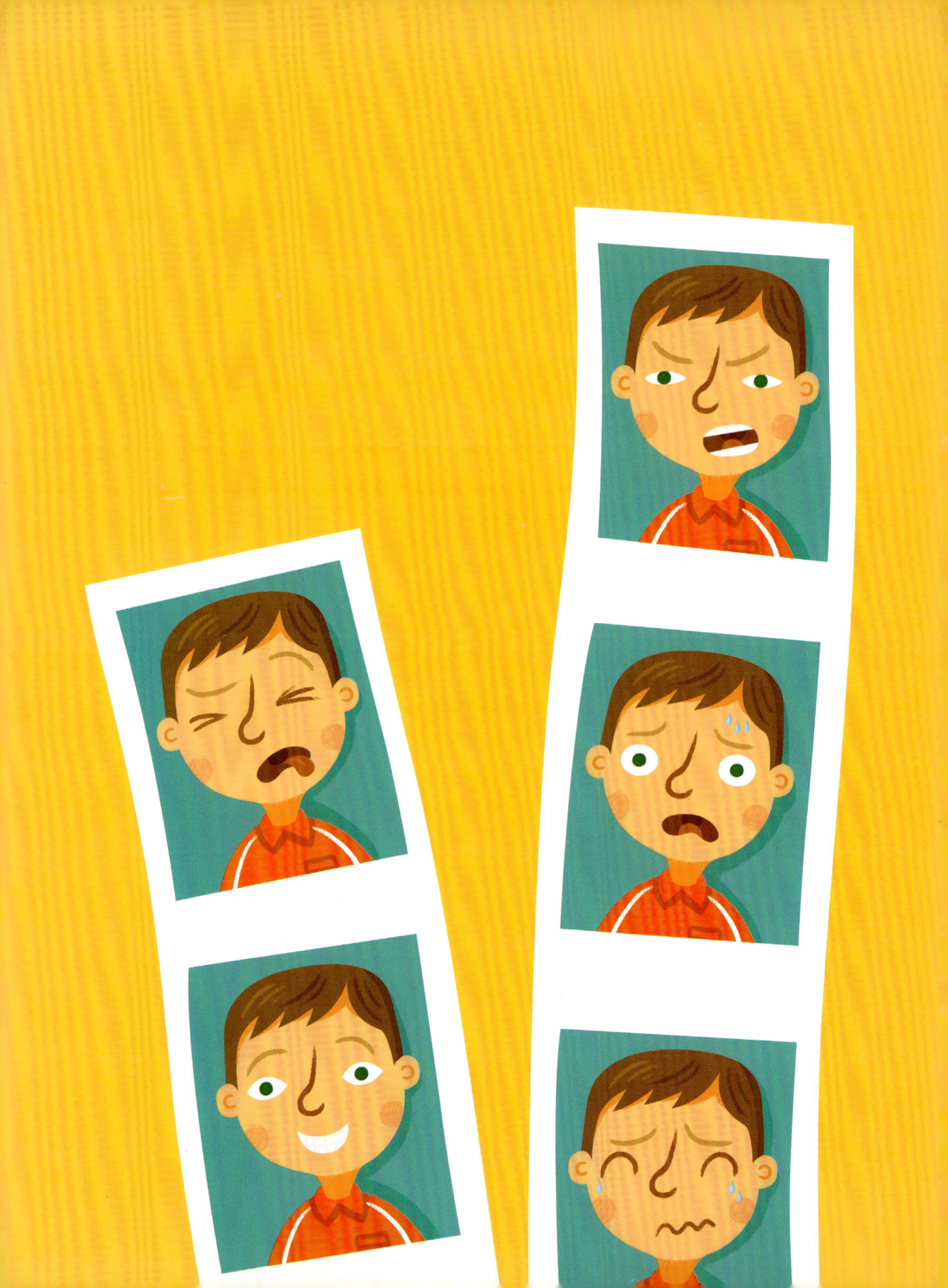

Emotions

As well as perceiving the outside world, your brain is continuously generating emotions and feelings such as happiness, sadness, and surprise. Emotions are important and can affect how you behave. Some emotions, such as fear, helped your ancestors survive long ago in the past. Today, your emotions can still help keep you safe as well as helping you to form memories and make decisions.

Emotions
Glossary

adrenal glands Glands in your body near your kidneys that release chemicals when you are scared.

amygdala A small, almond-shaped part of the brain deep in the temporal lobe, that is involved with emotions and memory.

EEG Short for electro-encephalogram, doctors and scientists use this to record electrical activity in the brain.

emotion A feeling, such as happiness, sadness, or fear, which occurs when your brain perceives certain changes in your body. Emotions can affect how you behave and the decisions you make.

exaggerated Made larger or more important than it really is.

filtering When talking about the brain, it means sifting through many thoughts and memories and removing or discarding those which do not matter.

limbic system A collection of different parts of your brain, deep inside it, that are involved in memory, emotion, and behavior.

neurons The technical term for nerve cells—specialized cells in the body that transmit signals in the nervous system.

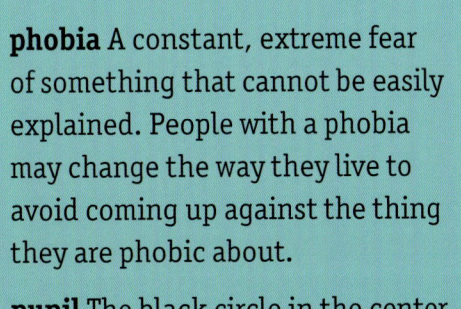

phobia A constant, extreme fear of something that cannot be easily explained. People with a phobia may change the way they live to avoid coming up against the thing they are phobic about.

pupil The black circle in the center of your eye, surrounded by the colored iris, which allows light to enter the eye.

thalamus Part of the brain that relays signals from the senses to other parts of the brain and connects different parts of the cortex together.

What are emotions?
... in 30 seconds

Many scientists believe that you have six basic emotions: fear, anger, happiness, sadness, disgust, and surprise. These are reactions to things you experience. They make a difference in how you understand the world and make decisions.

Emotions not only involve your brain and thoughts, they are bodily reactions that your brain senses. When you experience pleasure, your muscles tend to relax and your heart beats more slowly. Your brain recognizes the changes and gives the feeling a name—happiness!

Scientists believe emotions are triggered by the amygdala and other inner parts of the brain, which are together known as the limbic system. Emotions occur without you actively thinking about them. They usually happen quickly to prepare your body to take action, such as turning away in disgust and moving away from rotting food.

Of course, you have many other feelings such as pride, guilt, and love, but these are different from the basic emotions. They tend not to happen automatically, do not always involve bodily reactions, and often need you to think about people, objects, or events before they occur.

3-second sum-up

Your basic emotions are triggered by the brain and prepare your body to take action.

Emotions and memories

Did you know that strong emotions can affect your memory? For example, if you experience sadness at the loss of a pet, your brain pays full attention and takes note. The memory may be easy to recall in detail at a later date. When you recall an emotional event, you often remember not only what happened but also how you felt at the time.

The brain triggers your emotions and your body reacts by taking action.

You smell rotting food, may feel sick, and turn away in disgust.

Hearing a rude comment makes you angry and you might answer back.

Getting a high score on a test makes you happy and you want to repeat the experience.

A threat causes fear and you react to save yourself from harm.

Surprise at an unexpected gift! Your brain focuses all its attention on the gift to take in as much information as it can.

If you are sad, you may start crying.

Fight or flight
... in 30 seconds

One of your key emotions is fear. It is your body's early warning system. It picks up possible threats to your well-being and prepares you to take action to avoid harm.

When you experience fear, changes occur in both your brain and body. The thalamus passes on sensory signals to the amygdala (see page 15). The amygdala communicates with the front of your brain, asking it to analyze the threat. The amygdala also sends instructions to your nervous system and adrenal glands, which release chemicals that give your body a supercharging boost.

Your body speeds up and you become very alert. These actions prepare you for a big physical challenge ahead, such as escaping as fast as possible or using all your strength to fight off an attack. This is called your "fight or flight" response. People in the past relied on it to survive many frightening life-or-death situations.

Today, you are more likely to use the fight or flight response to avoid everyday dangers, from not taking a shortcut through a dark alley to changing direction when you see a fierce dog ahead.

3-second sum-up

Fear prepares you for a physical response to save yourself from harm.

3-minute mission Phenomenal phobias

An extreme and exaggerated fear of a certain object, creature, or situation is called a phobia. Can you match the phobia names to the right description?

Phobia: claustrophobia; haphephobia; agoraphobia; spectrophobia

Fear of: open spaces; mirrors; small, enclosed spaces; being touched

Answers on page 96.

When your senses detect possible danger, your body reacts and may trigger a flight or fight response.

The front of the brain analyzes the threat.

The pupils dilate (open wide) to let in as much light as possible.

Sweating increases to speed up heat loss before fighting or running.

The heart beats faster. It forces blood around the body more quickly, carrying glucose for energy and oxygen.

The lungs expand to take in more oxygen.

The muscles tense up, ready for action.

Sleep and dreams
... in 30 seconds

Do you know what you do more than anything else?
No, it's not eating, playing computer games, or watching TV . . . it's sleeping! By the time you reach 21 years of age, you will have spent approximately seven years of your life asleep.

Scientists are fascinated by sleep and what it does for us. They think it helps our bodies use less energy and to rest and recover after a day of activity. But your brain never fully rests. It remains busy throughout the night—EEGs of sleeping people show lots of electrical activity going on in their brains.

What is your brain up to at night? Many scientists think it is doing mental housework—encoding and linking memories, sorting the experiences of the day, and filtering out unnecessary information. Others think the brain's neurons may be recharging themselves, getting ready for the next day's challenges.

You sleep in a series of stages. Your dreams arrive mainly in one stage, known as "rapid eye movement." Scientists aren't sure why we dream, but many think it has to do with the brain making sense of your experiences that day and the memories it is cataloging.

3-second sum-up
Your brain stays busy as you sleep, both when you dream and when you don't.

3-minute mission **Keep a dream diary**

You need: • Notebook • Pen

As soon as you wake up each morning, write down what you remember about the dreams you had that night. Keep the diary for three weeks. Did any dreams or parts of dreams reoccur? If your dreams were all different, were there common themes?

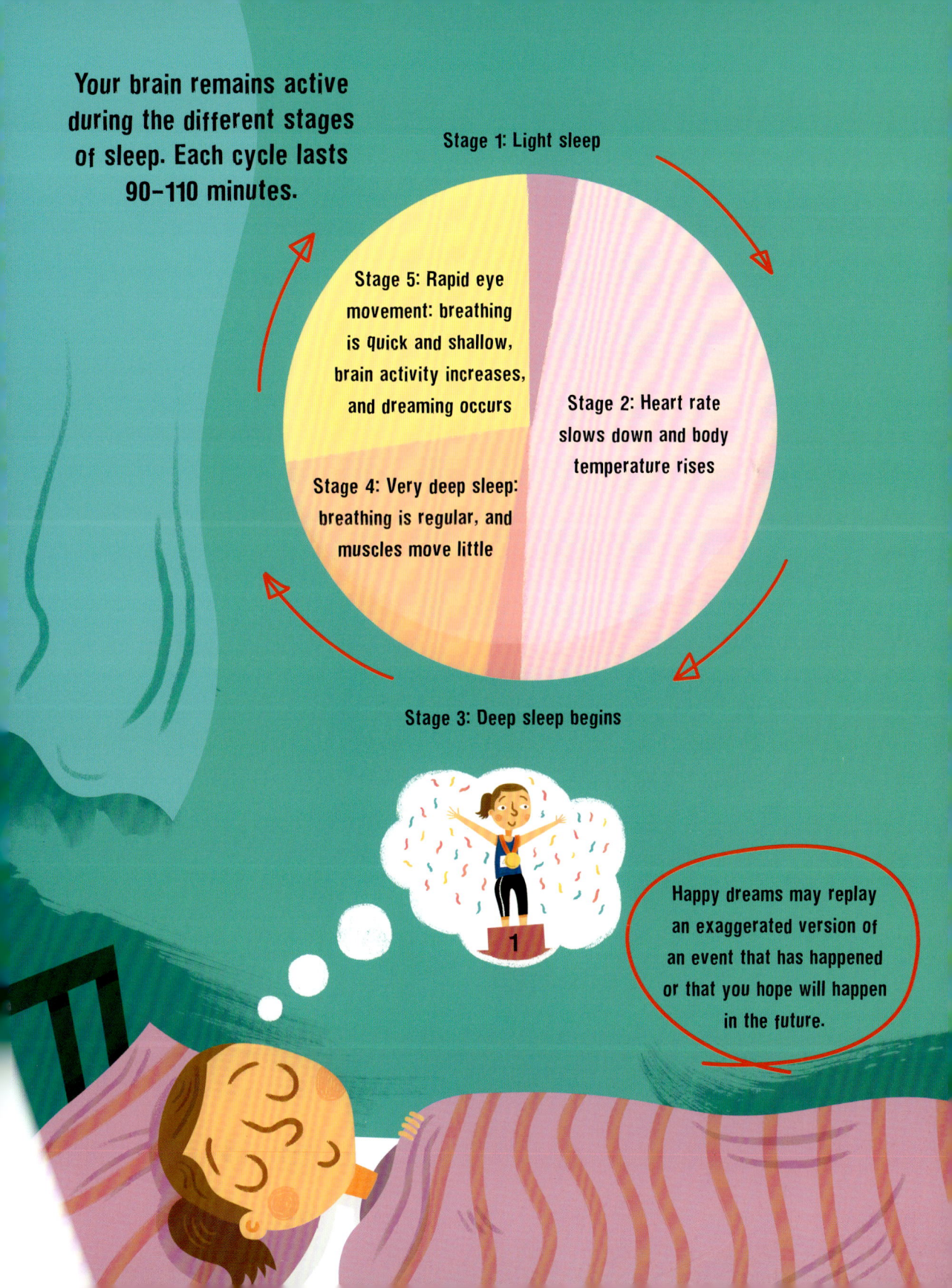

Your brain remains active during the different stages of sleep. Each cycle lasts 90–110 minutes.

Stage 1: Light sleep

Stage 2: Heart rate slows down and body temperature rises

Stage 3: Deep sleep begins

Stage 4: Very deep sleep: breathing is regular, and muscles move little

Stage 5: Rapid eye movement: breathing is quick and shallow, brain activity increases, and dreaming occurs

Happy dreams may replay an exaggerated version of an event that has happened or that you hope will happen in the future.

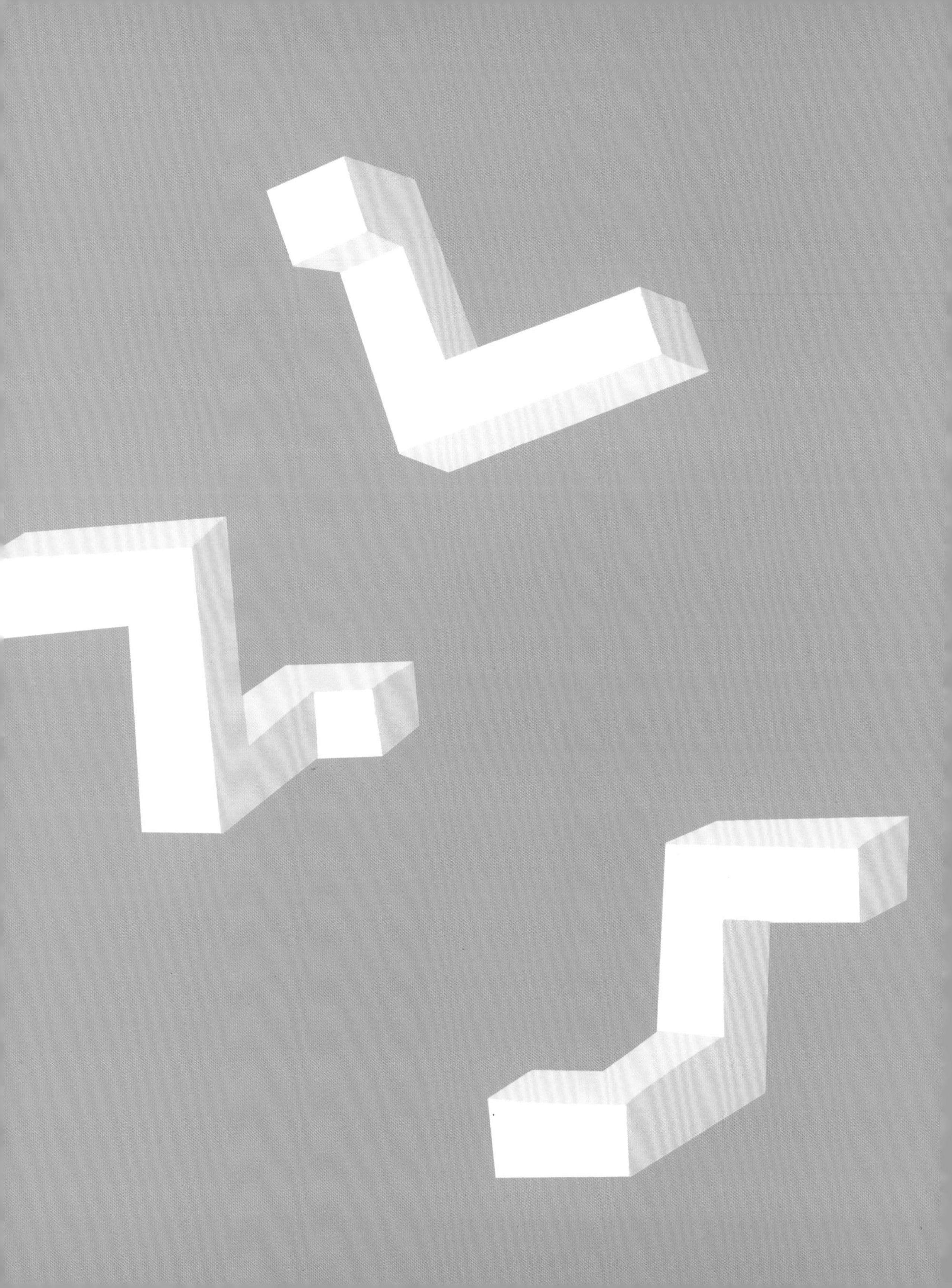

Brain skills

Your brain controls your body's systems, allows you to react to unexpected events, and stores all of your previous thoughts and experiences in memory. But it offers you much, much more. Your brain gives you the skills to plan ahead, to understand and communicate with others, and to make many different decisions. It also allows you to imagine things not as they are but in other ways, and to come up with creative solutions to problems.

Brain skills
Glossary

AI Short for artificial intelligence, this involves designing machines and computer programs that can perform tasks that normally require human intelligence.

communicate To pass on or share information with others.

coordinate To make the different parts of your body work well together.

creativity The ability to come up with new and original ideas.

distraction Something that interrupts your attention and stops you from concentrating on something else.

interpersonal intelligence Being able to understand others, to put yourself in their situation, and to deal with people successfully.

intrapersonal intelligence The ability to understand yourself, your wants and fears, and knowing what makes you happy or unhappy.

language A system allowing communication of thoughts and feelings through voice sounds, gestures, or written symbols.

logic The use and study of reasoning.

manipulate When talking about the brain and spatial awareness, it means to be able to handle, rotate, and view visual images from different angles and viewpoints.

spatial awareness To have a good understanding of objects, distances, and space around you.

three dimensions (3D) If you can see things in 3D, you can see they have not only height and width but also depth.

vocabulary All the words understood and used by a particular person.

Types of intelligence
... in 30 seconds

Intelligence is all about how people are able to learn, think, understand ideas, make decisions, and adapt to things around them. Intelligence isn't just about how good you are at school work, so you might be smarter than you think!

Some scientists split intelligence into many different types. Most people are more intelligent in some ways than others. Some people have great **musical intelligence**. This is the ability to identify different sounds, notes, and rhythms, and to pick up tunes easily.

Mathematical-logical intelligence is the ability to deal with numbers, sums, and equations. If you have this form of intelligence, you may also be good at recognizing patterns and analyzing certain types of scientific problems.

Not all types of intelligence are about music, numbers, or problems. Several are about people. **Interpersonal intelligence** is your ability to understand others, to put yourself in their situations, and to deal with people successfully. **Intrapersonal intelligence** is how good you are at understanding yourself and what makes you tick.

3-second sum-up

Intelligence comes in different forms, including the ability to learn and to understand yourself and others.

3-minute mission Math puzzle

Test out your mathematical intelligence by trying to solve this tricky math puzzle.

Use the numbers 1, 2, 3, 4, 5, and 6 to fill the six gaps in the math equation below. You should use each number just once. Make sure the equation is correct!

$$\_\,\_\,\_ \div \_ = \_\,\_$$

Answer on page 96.

Different types of intelligence allow people to be good at different things.

People who can juggle show great kinesthetic intelligence—the ability to control their body and coordinate the movements of its parts.

Being a good salesperson and being able to deal well with people requires good interpersonal intelligence.

Use your mathematical intelligence to figure out this puzzle.

Study the two sets of balanced scales. How many apples will balance the third set? Answer on page 96!

Language intelligence
... in 30 seconds

Many creatures communicate with one another using calls or other signals, but our ability to learn and use complex language with a huge range of words and meanings seems to set us apart from other animals.

Language intelligence allows us to describe our thoughts, ideas, and experiences in great detail and pass on this information with ease. We can learn from verbal (spoken) instructions, written language, gestures, or visual information in books, magazines, or webpages.

If you have good language intelligence, you can understand information easily and get your point across well using writing and speech. You have a good vocabulary—a range of words you know, understand, and use. When thinking of what to say or write, your brain searches through your vocabulary, stored in memory, to pick out the words with the right meaning.

When you were a toddler you probably had a vocabulary of only 100–200 words. At this age, your brain was very good at picking up new words. By the time you hit high school, you will probably have a vocabulary of 10,000–15,000 words. Amazing . . . excellent . . . fantastic!

3-second sum-up

Language is a system for communicating with others through speaking, writing, or symbols.

3-minute mission Word puzzle

Find the odd word out in each row and explain why it doesn't fit.

1 kick, bounce, push, jump, sew, girder, run, pull
2 shiny, glistening, jagged, digging, ugly, furry, dirty, narrow
3 dangerous, risky, hazardous, secure, lethal, threatening, unsafe, perilous

Answers on page 96.

Language can be verbal, visual, written, or in gestures, and allows us to express our thoughts.

Quack! Quack!

Toddlers learn to speak.

Duck!

Animals communicate with each other too.

PARK MAP
Ice-cream stall closed today

Written language allows ideas to be passed on from one generation of people to the next.

Oh no, the ice-cream vendor is closed! What shall we do?

A map is a visual language, often accompanied by written words.

We use a lot of gestures and expressions to communicate.

Visual-spatial intelligence
... in 30 seconds

Your visual-spatial intelligence helps you understand and make use of the visual information your brain receives. You rely on it every day—from judging whether an object in another room will fit in a box to learning your way around a new school building.

Some people have excellent visual-spatial intelligence. They may be:
- good at solving visual puzzles such as jigsaw puzzles and mazes
- capable of understanding and interpreting graphs, charts, and pictures
- good at reading maps, finding their bearings, and following directions
- observant and quick to notice visual changes in places and people
- spatially aware—able to see and deal with spaces, objects, and distances in three dimensions (3D)
- good at drawing, sculpture, and technical drawing.

Designers, architects, engineers, and police officers inspecting a crime scene also rely on their ability to work visually. Many athletes need to judge the space around them and the position of other players.

3-second sum-up

Judging distances, shapes, objects, and images is part of your visual-spatial intelligence.

3-minute mission Match the pattern

Look at the following row of six circles. Without turning the book, can you figure out which one of the five circles, labeled A–E, matches the circle on the left?

A   B   C   D   E

Answer on page 96.

Good visual-spatial intelligence allows you to find your way around, judge movement and distance, and view objects from different angles in your mind.

Test your brain's ability to view 3D objects from different angles.

B

A

C

Which of these two objects are identical? Answer on page 96.

Athletes often need to understand the constantly changing position and movement of players and the ball around them.

Players are aware of their teammates' and opponents' positions.

The goalkeeper judges her position in the goal and how close the ball is.

Players judge the speed and direction of the moving ball.

Logic and problem-solving
... in 30 seconds

Your brain solves loads of problems and makes dozens of decisions every day, from figuring out equations to deciding what to wear. It uses various tools to perform these tasks, including ways of thinking known as logic.

Almost 900 years ago, a scholar called Ibn Rushd called logic: "The tool for distinguishing between the true and the false." Your brain uses logic to understand the connections between different pieces of information. You use logic every time you perform a math equation such as 56 - 18 = 38.

Reasoning is a system of thinking. It uses logic to work out a conclusion from known facts. A simple piece of reasoning, known as deduction, may involve the two facts "all birds have wings" and "a penguin is a bird." From these two facts, you can make the true conclusion that a penguin has wings. Deduction only works, however, if the facts are correct!

Logic and emotions are often used together to make decisions. Your emotions might influence you to pick options that increase your happiness or decrease fear, such as choosing the safest rather than the shortest way home.

3-second sum-up

Logic helps you solve problems and make decisions, assisted by your emotions.

3-minute mission Puzzle it out!

Logic puzzles can stretch and test your powers of reasoning and logical thinking. Here are two puzzles for you to solve.

1 Can you place six X's on a tic-tac-toe grid without making three in a row?
2 How do you cut a round birthday cake into eight equal-sized pieces with just three cuts?

Answers on page 96.

We use both logic and emotion to make decisions—like this boy deciding which route home to take.

HOME

It's a fact that route A is the shortest way home and I can walk.

But there's a fierce dog along the way, and I'm really scared of it.

But I can stop at the candy store on the way and buy a yummy candy bar!

But then I'd miss out on the candy bar.

A

SCHOOL

It's a fact that route B is longer than route A but shorter than route C.

B

C

It's a fact that route C is longer than A or B. But if I go that way I can get the bus home.

Creativity and invention
... in 30 seconds

Feeling creative? Whenever you make something new or develop your own version of something, you are exercising your brain's remarkable ability to be creative.

Creativity is a mysterious thing. Scientists don't think there is one single part of the brain that comes up with all of your brilliant, wild, and wacky ideas. Instead, creativity involves many parts of your brain, which may link ideas, thoughts, and memories together so that you can produce something new or different.

Creative skills are important in the arts, from writing poems and music to making sculptures, and they are also vital in science, business, and engineering. Many useful inventions, from the flexible straw to the trampoline—invented by 16-year-old George Nissen in the 1930s—relied on a burst of creative thought from the brain of their inventor.

How can you boost your creativity? There are lots of different ways. Some big thinkers, such as scientist Charles Darwin, found they were at their most creative when walking outside, away from distractions. The great physicist Albert Einstein said that some of his best ideas came to him in dreams. Other people find it helps to think visually and sketch out ideas.

3-second sum-up

Creativity is the ability to make new things or think up fresh ideas.

3-minute mission Be creative!

You need: • Small box • Paper clips • Rubber band • Drinking straw • String • Lump of modeling clay

On your own or with friends, see what you can build with these items. Then, imagine what you could construct if you had unlimited numbers of these items.

Creativity happens when information in different parts of the brain connects in ways that produce new ideas.

Associating things not normally linked together can sometimes lead to new inventions or ways of doing things.

Creativity can be as important in science and technology as in the arts.

Creating a new idea is just the start. You may need patience and lots of effort to make it a success.

Not all ideas work. In the 1800s, inventor Thomas Edison invented a couch made of concrete. It didn't catch on!

Artificial intelligence
... in 30 seconds

Can machines be built that are as smart as people?
That's the goal of artificial intelligence (AI). AI aims to create computer software or machines, such as robots, that are intelligent and can learn, act, and adapt, much like humans do.

AI has made progress. Some computers can outperform humans, but usually only at one task. World chess champion Garry Kasparov was beaten at chess by the Deep Blue computer in 1997, and in 2011 IBM's "thinking" computer Watson beat human champions of the *Jeopardy!* TV quiz show.

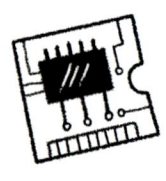

In some ways, your brain is like a computer. It needs energy to run, uses tiny electrical signals to communicate between different parts, and stores information in memory. Like a computer, your brain takes in data, processes it, and makes things happen.

But in many other ways, your brain is so, so superior. It is far more flexible, can perform many different types of jobs, and can think for itself. Your brain gives you an imagination and creative ways to solve problems, and it constantly reprograms itself. So far, no machine or device has come close to matching the power and skill of your brilliant brain.

3-second sum-up

AI aims to produce machines with the same flexible, creative intelligence as humans.

The wonders of robots

Robots are amazing machines. Many are able to work without people supervising them all the time. Some robots have dived the ocean depths, clambered into the mouths of volcanoes, or explored space. A number of robots can learn about their surroundings and change how they act. But today's robots rely on people to program them with instructions in the first place.

Scientists can create intelligent robots that can learn and carry out tasks, but they work quite differently from real people.

The human brain is better at understanding the outside world and coming up with new ideas.

The human brain is energy efficient, using about as much energy as a 12-watt light bulb, while IBM's "thinking" computer Watson uses 90,000 watts!

Robots are extremely good at performing the same task over and over again with accuracy.

Your creative, imaginative brain enables you to come up with many new ideas and ways of doing things.

Discover more

BOOKS

Body Works: Brilliant Brains by Anna Claybourne
QED Publishing, 2014

Brain Twisters by Clive Gifford
Ivy Kids, 2015

Eye Benders by Clive Gifford
Ivy Kids, 2014

Human Body: A Children's Encyclopedia
Dorling Kindersley, 2012

Thirty Days Has September: Cool Ways to Remember Stuff
by Chris Stevens
Buster Books, 2013

Train Your Brain To Be A Genius by John Woodward
Dorling Kindersley, 2013

Your Brilliant Body: Your Mind-Bending Brain and Nifty Nervous System
by Paul Mason
Wayland, 2015

DVDs – suitable for all ages

National Geographic: My Brilliant Brain
National Geographic, 2010

The Secret Life Of The Brain
http://www.pbs.org/wnet/brain
Fascinating video series exploring how the brain develops from baby to adult.

WEBSITES

Brain Bashers
http://www.brainbashers.com/puzzles.asp
A huge collection of word and number puzzles, logic puzzles, and optical illusions to challenge you.

How Stuff Works: The Human Brain
http://science.howstuffworks.com/life/inside-the-mind/human-brain/brain.htm
A good introduction to the human brain, its different parts, and how it works.

Kidshealth: Your Brain and Nervous System
http://kidshealth.org/kid/htbw/brain.html
A look at the different parts of the brain and how they work together.

Neuroscience For Kids
http://faculty.washington.edu/chudler/neurok.html
A massive website on the brain, senses, and nervous system, with experiments and activities.

Although every endeavor has been made by the publisher to ensure that all content from these websites is educational material of the highest quality and is age-appropriate, we strongly advise that Internet access be supervised by a responsible adult.

Index

acronyms **56**
adrenal glands **68, 72**
amygdala **10, 15, 70, 72**
anger **70, 71**
artificial intelligence (AI) **78, 90–91**
associations **56, 62, 65**
axons **26**

binaural hearing **40**
brain stem **10, 14, 15**

cells **10**
central nervous system **26**
cerebellum **10, 14, 15**
cerebrospinal fluid **10, 12, 13**
cerebrum **10, 14, 15**
chunking **56, 64, 65**
cilia **42**
cochlea **40, 44, 45**
connections, making **30–31**
corpus callosum **10, 15, 19**
cortex **10**
cranium **12, 13**
creativity **78, 88–9**
CT scanners **20**

dendrites **26**
disgust **70, 71**
distraction **78**
dreams **74–5**

EEG machines **10, 20**
emotions **67–73, 86**
endocrine system **26, 36–7**

fear **70, 71, 72–3**
filtering **68**
focus **40**
forgetting **62–3**
frontal lobe **16, 17**

glands **26, 36–7**
glucose **10, 22–3**

happiness **70, 71**
hearing **44–5**
hemispheres **18–19**
hormones **26, 36**
hypothalamus **10, 15, 36, 37**

illusory contours **52, 53**
intelligence **80–91**
interpersonal intelligence **78, 80, 81**
intrapersonal intelligence **79, 80**

kinesthetic intelligence **81**

language **79, 82–3**
learning **30–31**
lens **46, 47**
limbic system **68, 70**
lobes **16–17**

logic **79, 86–7**
long-term memory **56, 60–61**

mathematical intelligence **80, 81**
melatonin **36, 37**
memory **80–91**
meninges **11, 12, 13**
mnemonics **56, 64**
MRI scanners **11, 20**
muscles **26**
musical intelligence **80**

nervous system **32–3**
neurons **26, 28–9, 30**
neurotransmitters **26**

occipital lobes **16, 17, 46**
odorants **40, 42, 43**
olfactory bulbs **40, 42, 43**
optical illusions **50–51**
oxygen **11, 22–3**

pain **34, 35, 48, 49**
pareidolia **52**
parietal lobe **16, 17**
perception **41, 50–51**
peripheral nervous system **26, 32, 33**
phobias **69, 72**
pineal gland **36, 37**
pituitary gland **36, 37**
proprioception **41, 48**

pupils **34, 41, 46**

reactions, testing **32**
recall, testing **60**
reflexes **27, 34–5**
retina **41, 46, 47**
robots **90–91**

sadness **70, 71**
short-term memory **57, 58, 59**
shortcuts **52–3**
sight **46–7**
sleep **36, 37, 74–5**
smell, sense of **42–3**
spatial awareness **79, 84**
spinal cord **11, 27, 32, 34**
surprise **70, 71**
synapses **27**

taste **42–3**
temporal lobe **16, 17**
thalamus **11, 14, 15, 46, 72**
three dimensions (3D) **11**
thyroid **36, 37**
touch, sense of **48–9**

visual-spatial intelligence **84–5**
vocabulary **79, 82**

Answers

Page 12 Egg head

The egg in the container with water will survive because the water protects it.

Page 50 Test your brain

1. A rabbit or a duck. This image contains information your brain can interpret in two different ways.
2. The center circles are the same size. Your perception of the left circle is influenced by the larger circles around it, making your brain think it is smaller.
3. The lines are parallel. Your brain is tricked into thinking the lines travel away from each other.
4. They are the same color. The darker border influences your brain to think the right-hand square is brighter and lighter.

Page 72 Phenomenal phobias

Claustrophobia	Fear of small, enclosed spaces
Haphephobia	Fear of being touched
Agoraphobia	Fear of open spaces
Spectrophobia	Fear of mirrors

Page 80 Math puzzle

162 ÷ 3 = 54

Page 81 Types of intelligence

1 pineapple weight = 2 bananas
1 banana weight = 2 apples
So 1 pineapple + 1 banana = 6 apples
Values are Pineapple = 4, Banana = 2, and Apple = 1

Page 82 Word puzzle

1. girder. It is a noun (naming word) and the others are all verbs (doing words).
2. digging. It is a verb (doing word) and the others are all adjectives (describing words).
3. secure. It is an antonym, or opposite, of the rest of the list of words.

Page 84 Match the pattern

D.

Page 85 Three-dimensional objects

A and C.

Page 86 Puzzle it out!

1.

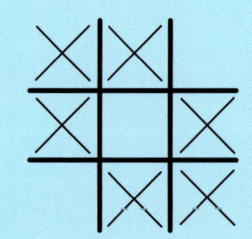

2. Make one horizontal cut by slicing sideways through the middle of the cake, then two right-angled cuts through the top of the cake.